SEXTS, TEXTS & SELFIES

Susan McLean is Australia's foremost expert in the area of cyber safety and young people. Susan works with a range of organisations, including schools, adolescent psychologists, mental health bodies and medical practitioners; elite sporting groups such as the AFL and Cricket Australia; and law firms and businesses. She is a member of the National Centre Against Bullying (NCAB) Cybersafety Committee and the Federal Government's Cybersafety Working Group (CWG) and is a Stay Safe Online ambassador. Susan was a member of Victoria Police for twenty-seven years.

cybersafetysolutions.com.au

SUSAN McLEAN

SEXTS,

TEXTS

& SELFIES

VIKING
an imprint of
PENGUIN BOOKS

VIKING

UK | USA | Canada | Ireland | Australia
India | New Zealand | South Africa | China

Penguin Books is part of the Penguin Random House group of companies
whose addresses can be found at global.penguinrandomhouse.com.

Penguin
Random House
Australia

First published by Penguin Group (Australia), 2014

Text copyright © Susan McLean 2014

Cover design by Adam Laszczuk © Penguin Group (Australia)
Text design © Penguin Group (Australia)
Author photograph by Andre Sawenko
Typeset in Adobe Garamond Pro by Samantha Jayaweera, Penguin Group (Australia)
Printed and bound in Australia by Griffin Press, an accredited ISO AS/NZS 14001
Environmental Management Systems printer

National Library of Australia
Cataloguing-in-Publication data:

McLean, Susan (Susan Gay)
Sexts, texts and selfies / Susan McLean.
9780670077885 (paperback)
Cyberbullying. Cyberbullying--Prevention. Internet and children.
302.34302854678

penguin.com.au

CONTENTS

INTRODUCTION

There is nothing easy about being a parent. Babies do not come with instruction manuals and we often rely on our own parents, friends and others to assist us in this wonderful journey we are undertaking. It is filled not only with fear, trepidation and worry, but also exhilaration, love and pride. It is a journey like no other and sometimes we all need help to navigate the highway of parenthood.

Enter the internet and a million different devices, and suddenly there's a whole new world to navigate – complete with delights, challenges and obstacles. Collectively, we don't have generations' worth of knowledge about how to keep our children safe online, but together, today, we can make sure their online experiences are safe ones. As parents, you need to understand your child's digital world, because *their* tech skills, together with *your* maturity, life experiences and knowledge, are going to make this parenting journey into cyberspace as successful and stress-free as possible. After all, technology itself is not the issue; it is the user of the technology who creates the risks and dangers.

This book is for you, right now. It will tell you everything you need to know about the digital world and how it affects your children: what your children are doing online, what they shouldn't be doing, what you can do to help them get the best out of technology and, most importantly, what you can do to keep them safe.

Our children are digital natives, born into a world where they are constantly surrounded by it. They cannot imagine life before mobile phones, iPads or the internet. Smart devices and social media sites have become part of our children's lives and they strongly influence how our children create, share and exchange information with others.

Despite all the great things about cyberspace, the online world does create some problems for children. For example:

- They are tech-savvy but lacking in 'actual knowledge' and cognitive development.
- It is their *primary* form of socialising and communicating.
- They have no fear of technology or cyberspace.
- It is extremely important for them to be connected.
- There is enormous pressure to conform.

While kids today are supremely tech-savvy, we shouldn't confuse this with actual knowledge, an understanding of dangers and risks, cognitive development and maturity. Your children will most probably leave you for dead when it comes to tech use, but what you *can* assist them with is real knowledge about what cyberspace is, what happens there, how to identify and deal with problems, how to stay safe and how to use some basic common sense. Sadly, from what I see on a daily basis, common sense is just not that common.

The reality is that the concept of common sense is foreign to many people, including adults, and when we are dealing with young, vulnerable, impressionable and hormonal adolescents whose brains are still very much a work in progress, it is often impossible for them to think things through the same way an adult would. They do not have the ability to pause and reflect on the consequences of their actions before doing something and because they are young, they do not have the life experience or maturity to understand the consequences even after they have been explained to them. This is why parents are so important in this online journey.

As a parent of three children (young adults now), I have had to deal with this head-on for the past seventeen years, from when my eldest was first introduced to online technology at school. Like most 'old people' I had no idea, was not particularly interested and hadn't really put much thought into how my parenting would change in the digital era.

Our first computer at home did not even connect to the internet; we used it only to type documents or perhaps insert a disk to play a game. We had planned to wait until our eldest was at secondary school before we got a computer at home as we really thought it was unnecessary until then. However, we relented and purchased one when she was in Grade 3, as it was apparent to us that technology was an important tool and we needed to embrace it as our daughter was being taught to do at school. This meant that our first-born was nine years old when technology entered our house. Our youngest had access from the time he was able to click a mouse. I am convinced he was born with an iPhone in one hand and a MacBook in the other. He is never 'not connected'. How times have changed! Although only six years separate my oldest and youngest children (with one in between), they are a generation apart when it comes to technology. The generation gap in this instance is not twenty to twenty-five years; it's around only five years, which makes keeping up with technology – the good and the bad – even harder. What we as parents may have proudly mastered last month is probably on the way out by this month, or in the not-so-distant future.

My career began when I joined Victoria Police on 15 March 1982. Like most young and keen constables, I loved to catch a crook. Any crook would do, but there was a thrill and deep satisfaction when you managed to arrest someone for a more serious crime. In those days crimes happened in the real world, a concrete environment. My early career saw me stationed at Fitzroy, which was a particularly busy inner-suburban Melbourne station. It was renowned for having more pubs per square kilometre of any police area. Cybercrime had not been invented at that point and manual typewriters were the order of the day.

Fast forward to 1994 when I was stationed in the outer northern suburbs of Melbourne, a relatively new and rapidly expanding area. I was part of the Police Schools Involvement Program (PSIP), which put police officers into local schools to provide positive interaction with local kids and to break down the barriers. The aim was also to use education to prevent kids from committing offences, being proactive rather than sitting and waiting for a problem and then trying to fix it. This was something that I was passionate about, and still am.

It was while running the PSIP program at this police station that my journey into cyberspace really began. I took my first report of cyberbullying as a Victoria Police officer in February 1994. I can still remember the phone call from a local Year 8 coordinator asking me to attend the school as he had a group of Year 8 girls who required, in his words, 'the police talk'. I arrived at the school having no idea what these girls had done. The teacher started to discuss the internet and I thought he was just making small talk. In 1994 I did not own a mobile phone; nor did I have the internet at work, and I rarely – if ever – used it at home. Then he said, 'These girls have been mean online.'

What? I remember my response was something like, 'Can you do that?' and 'That's not nice!' This was all I could think of saying. I didn't even know if a crime had been committed. As a police officer I had no idea and, worse still, as a parent, I was thinking, was this ahead for me?

To this day, that first case of cyberbullying is up there with the most serious I have dealt with. The girls had had a falling out and one wanted to get back at the other. The offender (for want of a better title) visited an adult sex chat room and posted an ad: 'If you want free sex, please contact this girl . . .' and included the name, address and phone number of the classmate she no longer liked. She could not have foreseen the consequences for the victim and her family. A stream of men came knocking on the door looking for the thirteen-year-old girl with her very kind offer of free sex. The family had to temporarily move to a motel and I had my cyberbullying baptism by fire. I honestly had no idea how to handle it but muddled through the best I could. I realised I needed to learn, and so I did.

Later in my career, I was called to deal with quite a comical issue involving a deputy principal. This person was tech-savvy and had embraced technology in her role but had chosen not to have a social networking page. On arriving at school one Monday, several staff commented to her that it was great she was now on Facebook. She replied that she was not and thought nothing of it until recess, when even more staff congratulated her on joining. She called the school's IT person and asked him to investigate why everyone thought she had a Facebook page. It quickly became apparent that one of the students had set up an account in her name, used her picture from the school website, made up a date of birth, then sent friend requests to all the staff, all of whom accepted her invitation, not realising that a student was behind it. This meant that the student had had access to many of the staff's Facebook pages for a whole weekend. What upset the deputy principal most was the fact that the student had put her age at sixty-five, when she was only in her early fifties! No real harm done, but it shows how anyone can be anyone online.

My journey to educate and research has taken me around the world, studying in both the USA and the UK. The more I learned, the more I wanted to learn, and it was clear to me that cybersafety was going to become a significant problem here in Australia, just as it had been in countries with much larger populations.

This book is based on all these years working in cyberspace as a police officer, my experiences as a mother to three highly tech-savvy children, my international study and research, and my current role that sees me in a school somewhere in the world almost every day, dealing with online issues, often providing initial crisis management, advice and solutions through the vast networks I have established with key online organisations.

I hope this book becomes your instruction manual for parenting in the digital space. I don't profess to know it all . . . but I want to share what I do know. We are all in this together. I often use this Donald Rumsfeld quote to explain the concept of cyberspace to others:

> There are known knowns. These are things we know that
> we know. There are known unknowns. That is to say, there
> are things that we know we don't know. But there are also
> unknown unknowns. There are things we don't know we
> don't know.

Begin the journey with me, and learn what you don't know you don't know. Good luck!

CHAPTER 1

SO WHAT'S IT ALL ABOUT?

Young people see the internet and mobile phone technology as a lifeline to their peer group. Whether we like it or not, it is a very real part of their life. But that same technology can also expose them to the following:

- inappropriate content
- cyberbullying
- sexting
- online grooming
- identity theft.

The perceived anonymity of the internet gives many young people a sense of bravado, allowing them to engage in behaviours that they would not consider in the real world. Most kids think they know it all . . . that they *won't* make a poor choice and they *will* be able to sort out the good from the bad. Kids don't always realise that making a poor choice online can be catastrophic, that they can't undo what they did, nor can they erase it. They do not understand that once you press the button to send, enter or upload, it is almost impossible to erase. There is no 'undo' button in cyberspace.

There is strong research evidence to suggest that adolescents in general, and male adolescents in particular, are developmentally less able to make informed decisions about personal safety and security than adults. The fact that they are tech-savvy does not compensate for their still-developing brain and their lack of maturity and life experiences.

Ten things you should know about cyberspace

So what are the important facts to consider when talking about tech issues with your children?

1. Respect and responsibility

If most technology users exercised respect and responsibility, we would have far fewer online issues to deal with. The basic ideology behind online use should be that each person has respect for themselves and others and uses technology responsibly. This is not a difficult concept; it comes down to common sense and common decency. It is simply impossible to hurt someone online or break a law by being respectful and responsible.

We need children to pause momentarily and ask themselves, Is what I am about to do online respectful of myself and/or someone else, and is it a responsible use of technology?

2. Cyberspace is a public place

Regardless of where you go, what you do or how you set up your accounts, the reality is that everything you do online is in the public domain. There is often a big difference between what you *intend* to happen with that text you send or photo you post and what actually occurs. Every online communication can be traced, found and then reposted or used again, with or without your permission.

Even if you have your accounts set to the highest level of privacy and security, the content is still accessible to those who know how. The notion of *privacy* online does not really exist; a better word to use is *security*. You can have a high level of security but never total privacy. Remember, even if a random member of the public cannot see the content initially, you have to consider that one of your 'friends' may intentionally or inadvertently share the content.

No-one really knows what cyberspace will look like in the future or how and where our information will be stored. We don't know whether sites will change their terms and conditions of use, or whether information we assumed was stored securely will somehow find its way into circulation. As many high-profile people around the world have found in recent times, if there is a digital copy of something, it will resurface when you least want or expect it. No-one has any way of knowing the full extent of what has been recorded about them, where all the tagged pics have ended up and even who will be able to access information that today is protected but may not be in the future. The best insurance policy is to think before you post in order to limit what might be out there ready to damage a reputation or ruin an opportunity twenty or thirty years down the track.

3. Nothing can be totally deleted – your content is permanently online

While the undo button can solve myriad issues, or the recycle bin or trash on your computer will keep deleted items until it's emptied, even when you've deleted an item, a computer expert can retrieve almost anything. Regardless of whether you can find something after you have deleted or 'lost' it, the fact remains that *it is still there somewhere*.

The same goes with mobile phones. A record of most things you send and receive are recorded and saved, and can be handed over to law enforcement if requested (by a clearly defined legal process). Even deleted messages on a smart phone can be found, unencrypted and transcribed back to a readable format by forensic technical experts. Search engines are like the tentacles of an octopus reaching out in all directions and gathering everything in their path. It will always be out there somewhere!

4. You are never anonymous online

No matter what you call yourself, no matter what accounts you set up, you are never truly anonymous online. There is of course a perception of anonymity, where you can hide behind a fake account or name or use an avatar, but if someone really needs to work out who is behind a phone number, blocked or not, or who started an account, it can be done. Police worldwide have the ability to obtain and serve warrants on websites, telcos and ISPs and force them to hand over the identity information required when investigating a criminal offence using technology.

5. You always leave a digital footprint

Everywhere you go online leaves a trace behind. Your digital footprint makes up your digital reputation so you do need to think about the sites you visit, what you post, the accounts you have and who you hang out with online. If you are going to do the wrong thing using technology, it will only be a matter of *when*, not *if* you get caught. (See also Chapter 3: Your Child's Digital Reputation.)

6. Manners maketh the man...or woman

Manners are important. They are important in the real world and they are equally important online; it's known as 'netiquette'. So what are the basics you need to teach your children?

- Remember that words do not convey facial expressions or emotion, so be aware of your tone.
- Even when using emoticons, things can easily be taken the wrong way.
- Caps lock equals shouting, so please don't.
- If you wouldn't swear in front of Nanna, probably best not to swear online.
- Don't send a text or email when you are overtired, emotional, angry, upset or drunk. If you can't calmly pause and reflect prior to sending it, then leave it till the morning.
- Treat others as you would like to be treated and remember, once its sent, it's out of your control.
- A good rule of thumb is that if you couldn't or wouldn't say it to a person's face or on a street corner, then it probably shouldn't be online.

7. Passwords must never be shared

As basic as the concept of not sharing your password is, you would be amazed at just how many children do just that. I am not talking about you, the parent, knowing your child's passwords; I am talking about kids, using passwords as a type of currency, in order to be considered another person's best friend forever (BFF). Kids want to be a BFF and to have a BFF, and if it's as simple as sharing a password then kids do it without thinking. They assume they can trust their friends, when in reality, sometimes it's their friends who will betray them. We also know that online predators who become a child's BFF online will often be given password access to accounts, which can lead to blackmail and other more sinister issues. Teach your children that passwords are a secret that they only share with Mum or Dad and that they should tell you if anyone asks for their password, or if they have mistakenly given it to someone else.

8. There is no such thing as a safe website or app

Many sites, especially those aimed at children, promote themselves as 'safe'. This often lulls parents into a false sense of security, believing that the site or app has an inbuilt safety setting to protect their children. While some sites are far safer than others, due to a range of security or restriction settings on offer, they only partially assist in providing a safer environment. When it comes to safety, all sites rely on two things:

- the security settings being used
- the honesty and intention of the user.

As we know, there are plenty of people in the real world happy to prey on the vulnerable to satisfy their perverted desires. Even other children know that they can set up accounts quickly and easily and use these to cyberbully others. Allow your children to use sites that you approve of, but do so with the knowledge that anyone – good, bad, old, young and everyone in between – may be there as well. There is no such thing as a *safe* website, just a *safe* user.

9. Anyone can be anyone online

It really is as simple as deciding who you want to be. Visit a site, fill in the gaps truthfully or otherwise, and away you go. Despite what sites tell you, there is no way to verify the details of the account holder and plenty of people lie online for a variety of reasons. Teach your children that just as some people lie in the real world, some people lie online and there is no way of really knowing if a person is who they say they are.

If an older male approached your child at the shops and said that they were fourteen years of age, it would be obvious the person was lying. Online, it is much easier to hide behind a screen and pretend. Predators will go to extraordinary lengths to make contact with children: they can use voice-changing software to make them sound like a young girl or boy; and the webcam might show a young boy or girl who has been paid to sit there and pretend to be the person speaking.

10. There are laws in cyberspace

If it's a crime in the real world, it's probably a crime online too. There are specific laws that are applicable to cyberspace and technology misuse, and often police do not have to prove intent. The fact that the act has taken place means the crime has been committed. A look at the law from an international perspective shows that while there are some slight differences, if it's an online crime in one country it most probably is in another country. Ensure that your children know it can be a criminal offence to misuse technology or to bully or harass someone online. Tell them that the exchange of naked 'selfies' or other sexually explicit images by those under the age of eighteen years is considered to be child pornography. The civil law of defamation also applies online. (See also page 146: Cyberspace and the law.)

CHAPTER 2

COMMON SENSE BEGINS AT HOME

Whether or not your house has all the latest gadgets, your child *will* be using tech devices at school, at a friend's house, the local library – the list goes on – so it is very important that you have some information to get you started with parenting in the digital space. What can children actually do online? How can I keep them safe? How should I manage technology in my home?

Being an effective parent in the twenty-first century does require an understanding of technology. It is not a fad that is going to go away. Your kids will not simply 'get over it' and, like everything else, you need to be able to talk to them about all online issues. The reality is, your children have already embraced it in full or will soon. When it comes to technology, be informed, be empowered and be in control.

Real-world parenting is the same as cyberworld parenting

Most parents get their head around the need to parent in the real world quite well. They actively encourage their children to behave well, make sensible decisions, obey rules and laws, not talk to strangers and so on, but when it comes to parenting online, somehow it is not treated with the same seriousness or even seen as necessary. Read the following examples and consider your responses:

- Your child begs you to let him/her go to a gathering at a friend's house. You know the parents will be away but your child tells you that the friend's older brother will be home with some mates and that it will be fine. Your child tells you that *everyone else* is going because *their* parents *trust* them and they will be the *only one* not allowed.

- Your child wants a fifteenth birthday party. You are quite happy for this to happen, provided it is limited to thirty people. Your child is fine with this but then tells you that there will be alcohol and asks if that is okay. It is clearly *not okay* with you, and you tell them that at this party there will be no alcohol. But no-one will come, is the reply.

- Your child is eleven years old. Many of their friends seem to have unsupervised access to the internet and are allowed to have accounts on sites that have clear age restrictions. You cannot understand the other parents (many of whom you know and consider to be good parents) allowing their kids to have accounts on sites like Instagram, Kik, Facebook and Snapchat, which have age restrictions of 13+. Your child begs you to allow them to have an account too. They only really want Kik and Instagram just to chat to their friends and share pictures with each other. 'Please, Mum/Dad, please!'

The majority of parents would have no hesitation in saying no to their child going to the unsupervised party, regardless of who else was attending, nor would they waver and allow alcohol at a fifteenth birthday party, but when we are talking about online access, some parents get all wishy-washy. They won't or don't say no; won't or don't acknowledge that online issues are serious, and take the easy way out by allowing their children to use these age-restricted sites. Many justify their decisions with, 'I insist I am their friend and I supervise,' or, 'I'm just getting them ready for when they turn thirteen,' or my favourite: 'I don't want them to miss out.' So I ask you these questions:

- Do you take your child to a hotel or provide them with alcohol, 'just to get them ready'?
- Do you let them drive a car, 'just to get them ready for their L plates'?
- Do you say yes to every request, dangerous or not, 'just so they do not miss out'?

Of course you don't. Regardless of what everyone else does, any problems that arise will be for you and your child to deal with: the fallout, the hurt or embarrassment, and any legal issues. Most parents underestimate the potential for problems online, but learn very quickly afterwards. Hindsight is a wonderful thing. Kids will make mistakes online just as they do in the real world; but it is our role to help prevent that.

Start the conversation

Maintaining open and honest conversation is the key
to minimising many online issues. The longer you wait,
the harder it will become.

Here are some tips to help make these conversations
work:

- Educate yourself about whatever it is you are
  going to discuss; knowledge is power.
- Be confident in your knowledge and ability
  as a parent.
- Start early or as soon as you are aware that you
  need to change things.
- Be in a calm mood, not angry, tired or irritable.
- Be honest with your child.
- Explain the 'why' behind the reason in an
  age-appropriate way. Expect some resistance
  from older children but stay strong.
- Enlist the support of other family members,
  grandparents and teachers. Working together
  makes life easier for all.
- Start out strict; you can always ease off a bit later.
  This is much better than being too slack and then
  trying to rein things in.
- Have clear rules, expectations and boundaries
  and explain why. (See page 141: the Online Family
  Safety Agreement.)
- If at first you don't succeed, try again;
  don't give up.
- Remember, it's not for the now, but for the future.

Start early with good online habits

Ensuring good online habits are formed early is paramount and, together with clear expectations on how the device is used, it will go a long way to making the online experience as safe and fun as possible for children, and as stress-free as possible for parents.

Cyberbullying, sexting, online grooming by predators, exposure to inappropriate content and damage to their digital reputation are the most common dangers that young people face online. Children can be both victim and perpetrator, so it is important you understand each issue individually. It is about risk. If you put yourself in a dangerous situation, then the risk will be greater.

Basic online safety rules to teach your child include the following:

- Never give out your name, address or age to someone who asks for it online.
- Never give out your email address or account details.
- Never have your age or year of birth in a screen name or email address.
- Don't use sexy, flirty or groovy email or screen names.
- Don't use sexy, flirty or offensive profile pictures.
- Anyone can be anyone online. People do pretend to be someone they're not.
- Tell Mum or Dad if someone online asks you questions that make you feel uncomfortable, or asks for your name and address.
- Tell Mum or Dad if a person online asks you to take your clothes off on a webcam (make this conversation age appropriate).
- If you don't know the person in the real world, no matter how nice they are to you, they are a STRANGER.

- Be polite online and don't use bad language or make nasty comments.
- Don't visit places online you are not allowed to go.
- If you are scared, upset or have seen something you know you are not allowed to see, leave the device and find an adult.
- Never set up an account or download an app without your parents' permission, and never if you are under the age restriction.
- Use technology with respect and responsibility and have fun.

Managing screen time at home

I am often asked how long a child should be online at night. How long should they be playing a specific game? What time should they log off at night? There is no one simple answer to these questions; the answers will depend on a wide range of considerations such as the age of the child, the website, the family situation and other influences such as illness, during holidays versus during the school term and so on. Most academic research around the world states the following guidelines are considered reasonable screen time (this includes television, iPod, iPad etc.) in relation to health and wellbeing:

under 2 years	No screen time
2–5 years	No more than 1 hour per day
over 5 years	No more than 2 hours' screen time total per day. This will change when in secondary school and most homework is done on an electronic device, but be aware of how long they are online. This means social online time must be limited.

For me, it's all about balance. Try to provide an even balance between the things that have to happen and the things that kids want to happen. Before you set a specific time limit to anything tech related, look at what else needs to be fitted in. Is there homework? After-school sport or music? Are you heading out to celebrate a family birthday? Is your child tired or unwell? All these things need to be considered every time. Schedules can be a good thing as long as you leave some down time. Set important guidelines and expectations for dedicated online time and the specifics of what that means. The minute technology use creates a negative impact for your family, you must act. Removal of technology privileges for breaking the rules is important, but so too is flexibility.

Simple tips for managing screen time:

- Set up an Online Family Safety Agreement (page 141) with room for consequences and rewards.
- Set a weekly schedule for each child and fill in the non-negotiable things first (sport, chores, etc.). Keep in mind the advisory time limits.
- Separate online homework time and online social time so they don't get mixed up.
- Schedule homework time each night (this can be dedicated homework, reading, revision and so on).
- Add a favourite TV show to the schedule, especially one that you watch as a family.
- Schedule dedicated outdoor play time or non-technology family time.
- Schedule their online play time (games, social network for older teens). This might be limited to thirty minutes on some nights, nothing on others and a little longer

on the weekend or holidays. Ensure that all the important things are completed first.

- Be clear, be firm, but be flexible. If your child's social time is missed one night because sport training ran late, then perhaps let them make up the time the following night. Allow an extra thirty minutes playing a suitable online game on the weekend for being good with their online time during the week. There must be some give and take.

- Ensure that all screens are switched off at least thirty minutes before bed. This ensures the brain can wind down sufficiently for sleep (electronic stimulation, such as from watching TV or using the computer, has been shown to interfere with both falling asleep and staying asleep).

It would be great if I could provide one cybersafety template that all families could take and use in their home, but this is not realistic. Every household is unique, with kids of different ages and stages, parents or carers with different levels of knowledge. Technology plays a very important role in everyone's lives, especially those of young people, but like all things, it needs to be balanced, managed, and age- and developmentally appropriate.

Outside influences

Your firstborn is usually going to be easier to manage in terms of many issues, including alcohol, partying, going out and technology use, as they don't have an older sibling doing things that may be okay for the older child, but inappropriate for them. If your eldest child is mainly friends with children who are also the eldest in the family, then they will not be exposed to as many risky behaviours at an early age either. If your child is the youngest or has friends with older siblings, the tables turn very quickly and it becomes harder to continually say no when they see their older brothers and sisters doing things. Young children do not understand the concept of age appropriateness. If a sibling does it, they want to do it too.

Make sure your children know that rules are rules and they apply everywhere. If they are not allowed to watch an M-rated movie at home, for example, then they cannot watch it at a friend's place. If there are certain sites they cannot visit at home, ditto at the friend's place. This is why parents need to work together to help each other, not work against each other. As always, though, your child may end up in a house with different values, different levels of supervision or none at all, or there may be an older sibling who will take great delight in showing the younger kids some 'fun' (scary or pornographic) sites.

If your child is going on a play date, consider the following:

- Do I know the other child's parents?
- Do I know what they will be doing?
- Do I know who will be home to supervise?
- Do they know my expectations for my child's use of technology?
- Let your child know they can always feign illness (gastro works well) and call you to come and get them if their friends are watching something scary, so they don't lose face.

These are important issues to sort out before the visit, rather than after something goes wrong. Make sure that the other parents know what your expectations are, and if you feel they do not respect your decisions, then don't let your child go. Ultimately your child's safety is in your hands and any resulting problems are going to have to be dealt with by you. Don't be afraid to say no.

In addition to supporting each other, parents also need to support their child's school. I feel particularly sad when a primary school principal tells me that some parents won't listen to them about the potential dangers of certain sites, and that they should obey the age restrictions (see also page 24) and get their underage kids off these sites. Parents pitted against parents or teachers helps no-one, especially the kids.

Here are a couple of comments from frustrated parents trying to do the right thing with their children and their online activities:

*It is very hard to be a parent surrounded by children given free rein on social media. My daughter had a slumber party for her birthday a few weeks ago. Four friends came and at one point they talked about Instagram. They said to my daughter, 'You are the **only one** who doesn't have it. You're the **odd one** out'.*

*I will not allow my children to use Instagram until they are of the correct age, but it makes it so much harder when I am opposed by so many other parents (some letting kids as young as nine have accounts). Makes me seem like the bad guy when I am actually trying to be the good guy for their future. Too many parents get lost in the **now**. They want to make their kids happy **now**, they want to give them what they want **now**. We are raising future responsible adults and our decisions need to be for the future, not the **now!**'*

Obey age restrictions

Many of my daughter's friends have Instagram – something
I emphatically do not allow my daughter to have due to
the alarming statistics regarding the use of images on the
internet.
Mother of eleven-year-old girl

While this mother's reasoning is quite legitimate, the *main* reason
an eleven-year-old should not have an Instagram account is because
the legal age to open one is thirteen years. This is pretty simple, and
non-negotiable. There are other issues that can be used to cement the
argument but when there is an age restriction, use it.

If you read or listen to any media reports about cyber issues and kids,
you will undoubtedly hear Facebook mentioned. Many parents hold a
deep-seated yet unfounded fear of the site and go out of their way to
ensure their children do not use it, often creating arguments that could
easily be avoided. In reality, Facebook has some of the best security settings of all the social networking sites. The problem is, kids don't know
about them, they don't use them, they still accept friend requests from
people they don't know and they don't always feel comfortable telling an
adult when things go wrong. Parents are often oblivious to the correct
security settings, and therefore cannot guide their child. (See page 38 for
Security Settings and page 133 for Parental Controls.)

The following is a relatively common conversation that I have with
parents:

Parent: *'My child is being cyberbullied online.*
         Can you help me?'

Me: *'Where is it occurring?'*

Parent:	*'Oh, it's not Facebook. There is no way my child is ever having a Facebook page! I know how bad that is.'*
Me:	*'So where is this happening?'*
Parent:	*'Instagram and Kik.'*
Me:	*'So what about the dangers and age restrictions on those sites?'*
Parent:	*'Oh, but aren't they the better ones? The ones for little kids?'*
Me:	*'NO!'*

Many parents compromise and allow their young children on sites that they either think are fine, or are told are okay by their children or other uninformed parents. Many have no idea that iPods and iPads allow social communicating via apps that are equally and in many cases far more dangerous. Just saying no is not going to work. Back up your reasons with well-researched facts and present these to your child. More often than not, they will understand.

Ensuring that you are well informed and confident to set rules and boundaries for technology use in your own home is just getting to first base; children will be using technology outside the home too, when you're not with them. Hopefully the values and knowledge you have instilled in your children will hold them in good stead when they are away from your watchful eye and the rules you have agreed on.

How do you check if a game/app or social media account is suitable for your child?

- Google the game/app and visit the website if there is one.
- Do a simple search online: 'Is XXX safe for kids?'
- Check online articles about the site/app/game to get a feel for it.

- Check for age restrictions (most are restricted to children thirteen years or older, but some state other older ages). These are legally binding as part of the terms and conditions of use.
- If it is a web-based game, check information in the parents' section, but take boasts of 'the safest place on the internet' or similar with a grain of salt.
- Check for security settings. Are there any? Can your child block people? Can they choose who to communicate with? Can strangers contact your child? How do you report problems?
- Read other reviews of the game/app. See what other parents are saying.
- Search for the game in the iTunes App Store for an age rating or the Google Play store for the maturity level. This rating is advisory only, much like TV show and movie ratings, but is a useful starting point. If an app is rated 17+ it is *not* suitable for young children. Just because others have it is not a reasonable or rational reason to allow your child to have it too.
- Check if 'free' is actually free. Most are free to download, but many want payment to advance in the game or to enhance the experience. Sort this out first and don't link your credit card to it for ongoing purchases. Kids don't understand cost. Several quick clicks can equal hundreds of dollars.
- Check a site like Common Sense Media (commonsensemedia.org) for really good up-to-date information about games and apps.
- Download or install the game and play it yourself. Set up an account on the social media site. Check security settings,

interactions and the content of the game, and decide if it's suitable for your child. Do they have the maturity to understand the interactions? Can others contact your child? Who tries to contact you?

Why be the parent who says no to age-restricted apps/games/sites?

- Because it is your responsibility to protect your child.
- Because it shouldn't matter what the other kids are doing.
- Because the internet is not a child's playground.
- Because hindsight is a wonderful thing.
- Because prevention is better than cure.
- Because it's not just phones and computers that connect to the internet. Tablets and many MP3 players like the iPod Touch and gaming consoles connect to the internet and allow apps and games to be downloaded.
- Because the grooming of children by paedophiles via apps in particular is becoming worryingly common.

Recently, I heard of several nine-year-old girls who were tricked into sending naked pictures of themselves to an online predator posing as a twelve-year-old boy on Kik. A couple of months later, the same thing occurred involving an eleven-year-old and a fifteen-year-old, and again the app of choice for the predator was Kik. This simply should not have happened, and if they had been supervised, they would not have become victims.

- Because if more parents said no and got their young kids off age-restricted sites, they would not be able to become a victim!

Just like the real world, cyberspace can be a dangerous place. We advise, guide and teach children about the real world, both good and bad. We don't focus on the negative but ensure that all bases are covered. The same concept should apply to parenting in cyberspace. You are not going to be able to offer 100 per cent protection in the online world, just the same as we cannot protect our children 100 per cent in the real world, but we have to get close.

Stay strong. Knowledge is power and as you navigate this book, it will all fall into place and you will have the knowledge to successfully parent in the digital space.

CHAPTER 3

YOUR CHILD'S DIGITAL REPUTATION

What would people find if they looked up your child's name online? What information has been cached in Google or another search engine? Their social networking profile, their profile pic, images or comments they have posted, even the 'friends' they have online, whether a real friend or not, can provide an insight into their character. Are there embarrassing or private pictures available via a Google image search? What about school newsletters, sporting club websites, dance competitions, competitive sport or awards obtained? What would people think of them when their first impression is their email address sitting in their inbox? What your child does online, what they post and what they are involved in is important, and will be even more important in the future.

For the children and adolescents of today, it will be their digital reputation that gets them over the line when competing for future opportunities. No longer will it suffice to have a couple of good referees who will say nice things about them, and it is no use waiting until they are searching for those opportunities to start to think about what their digital footprint looks like. As we've discussed, the internet is permanent and once something is out there, it is almost impossible to erase. Your child's digital footprint leads to his or her digital reputation: that is, what someone thinks about them based on what they find online.

I work with a range of organisations, including corporations, elite sporting bodies, media outlets and schools, and they all tell me that they research applicants more now than ever before. While ability and skills are important to them, so too is the perception of that person being decent and sensible. When a potential employer has to decide whether to give your child an opportunity, they will look them up online. If they don't like what they see, the opportunity will go to someone else with a better positive digital reputation. You can debate whether it is fair or not, whether people are being judgemental or jumping to conclusions, but this is reality.

A perfect example of this was when a Year 8 girl went off to audition for a particular music scholarship. The first part of the process was to prove that she was musically gifted and she easily made it through to the next stage of the process. When she was advised that she would need to come back for an interview she was told, 'Before you come back you need to google yourself and bring a printout of everything you find online that is related to you. We will be doing that too and we expect the two piles of printouts to match.' Already, in Year 8, she was going to be judged on what she had done online. It is never too early, and of course never too late, to think about what you are leaving behind online and what you may need to do to clean up your act.

What is a digital footprint?

Digital reputation was not even a concept as recently as ten years ago. No-one had been online long enough to have developed much of a footprint anyway. These days, it doesn't take long to build up a digital reputation.

Your child's digital footprint can be found in many places online:
- the wording of their email address
- their CV or an online application form
- their profile pic on social networking sites such as Facebook, Instagram or Twitter
- friends attached to their social networking pages ('guilty by association')
- 'likes' on their page
- content and images found in their name via a search engine such as Google (such as newsletter articles, journals, blogs or comments)
- places they hang out online, including blogs and all the different accounts they had or have
- the bluetooth name on their phone.

Social networking sites have exploded in popularity since MySpace launched in 2003. We have seen Facebook become the most popular social networking site in the world, with over 1 billion accounts. Add to this the current crop of popular apps such as Twitter, YouTube, Instagram, Kik, Snapchat, WhatsApp, Viber, FaceTime and iMessage, plus webcams and all the various web-based games and apps kids play, and you can see how easily a digital trail is laid. Your child's every move, pic, post, comment and phone call could be saved and stored, becoming part of their digital footprint that's unique to them and cannot be erased.

Your child, their reputation

Kids do not start their digital footprint themselves. That honour falls dubiously to their parents, who so often get caught up in wanting to share every proud and not-so-proud moment of their children's lives with others online, but who fail to acknowledge or even fully understand the long-term ramifications.

- Do you post ultrasound pictures of your unborn child?
- Do you blog or comment on every aspect of their life?
- Do you share fun (embarrassing or awkward) moments about your child with the rest of the world?

A recent study conducted by the London School of Economics and Political Science in consultation with EU Kids Online found:

> Many children below the age of nine were born with the first fragment of their 'digital footprint' already available online. These youngsters will be the first generation to experience the aggregated effect of living in a digital world over their whole lifetime. They will inherit their digital profiles as a work in progress from parents who often assume that the information they post carries the privacy and security levels available to them at the time of posting, or who did not consider such issues when they posted their child's ultrasound photos or doctors' reports.

Parents have always embarrassed their children, from the daggy dad wearing unfashionable clothes and making inappropriate remarks to the naked baby in the bath photos in their twenty-first birthday slide show. But the world is a different place today. Information once held privately in hard copy is now plastered online, on websites or in the

Recently a tweet showed up in my feed that caught my eye. 'My 2yo is nearly potty trained. Just missed!', tweeted the comedian. There was an accompanying picture of the evidence. It was gross and the accompanying comments by some of this person's thousands of followers were equally disturbing. On looking at the account further, I found many pictures of the young child in question, including her name, for all the world to see, *forever*. What was he thinking? Clearly not about the consequences for his child.

Cloud. Children have no say in the matter until they are old enough to understand and find it themselves, by which time it will be too late to do much about it, other than grin and bear it.

Before you post anything about your child online, stop and think for a moment:

- Do I have my location settings turned off so that the metadata cannot be read (metadata allows people to find the exact address of where the picture was taken)?
- Do I have the highest levels of security set for my account and only allow access to a small group of trusted friends (not public or friends of friends)?
- Would I want that picture or comment about me doing the same thing from my childhood on the front page of a national newspaper? Would I cringe with embarrassment? What would my employer think?
- Could the image be taken and used inappropriately or without my permission (to advertise a product or for an online predator to use and share)?

Parents are a vitally important cog in the wheel when it comes to the start of their child's digital footprint, although as the research above states, many are clearly not thinking long term. While the cute baby-in-the-bath photo has appeal to immediate family, it does develop a sinister connotation when found stored in an online predator's computer; likewise, when that cute little baby is an adolescent, will they appreciate that the image of them naked in the bath is online for everyone to see?

Also make sure that you know exactly what you are giving permission for when you sign 'permission to publish' forms for things such as school, sport or dancing. If you don't want your child splashed all over the internet, it is okay to say no. Permission to publish forms are often ambiguously worded and do not provide a clear idea of where the content is going to appear. The forms that some schools still rely on are from the days when the only place your child's image was going to be published was in the local paper or school magazine. School and sporting club newsletters are often now posted online for all to see, and most of these organisations have websites and social media pages also. Images of children under the age of thirteen years should not appear on a club or school's Facebook or Instagram account as they are restricted to people of thirteen years and above. Putting young kids' pictures on age-restricted sites can add to the temptation for children to set up a fake account in order to see themselves on the site. It is simply not a good look and reputable organisations do not do it.

Make sure that anything you sign in relation to the publication of your child's image or name addresses the following:

- **Where will the content go?** This must be listed clearly, including things such as a printed newsletter, online newsletter, website, Facebook page or local paper, and should provide an option for you to choose one only, a few, or none or all.

- **How will your child be referenced?** Do you want only their first name displayed, their first and last name, age, team's name? Are you happy for a picture to be published but no name? You must have the ability to choose what combination suits you.
- **Is the image going to be used for commercial purposes?** If they plan to use your child's image to advertise the organisation, they must obtain signed permission.

It is bad enough that children and adolescents need to think before they post, but to reach your teens and find that someone else, probably Mum or Dad, has already effectively built your digital footprint for you and that you cannot simply press the undo button and get rid of what you don't want would fill most teens with dread.

So what does a digital footprint look like and how can it be used to form your digital reputation?

Email

There is much debate about whether kids should have their own email address. For young children, I suggest letting them use a parent's email when starting out online. That way any rubbish that may come via email comes to the parent, and you have to log on for them, which means you get to see what they are doing. As much as you may want to trust your children, don't! It's not worth the risk. Keep control of the accounts until at least secondary school, and then gradually hand over control with clear rules about use. You still need to be involved.

Remember that many email accounts including Gmail and Yahoo! Mail have an age restriction of thirteen, although Yahoo allows a family account to be set up and Google has exceptions for use with educational apps.

Email account names: first impressions count

Do you know your child's email address? If not, why not? Kids can be creative, but not always in the best way. An email address is often the first thing people read about you, and we all know that first impressions count. What would someone assume simply by reading your child's email address? From my experience, I know girls often like to be sexy, flirty and groovy; they rock, they are a star, and often all together in the one email address. Boys often describe body parts, comment on their sexual prowess or use a play on words. Of course, not all children do this; most are happy just using their name, a combination of their name, a pet's name or a nickname, but don't just assume. Check them out.

A Melbourne teacher sent a job application to a school principal from her email address bigtits@xxxxx.com; sadly it did not add to her credibility or promote her teaching ability. Last year I got an email from ruby_pedo@ xxxxx.com, a journalism student wanting to interview me for an assignment. I began by checking that pedo was not part of her surname, then asked why she chose it. Her reply: 'OMG it's really bad isn't it? It's an old one and my uni inbox was full so I just used it. I DIDN'T THINK!!!' This just about sums it up . . . they don't always think.

For girls, an email address such as hotgroovychicksexybabe97@ xxxxx.com might be fun among your friends and I am sure Facebook wouldn't be fazed if you joined with this address, but a prospective employer may think otherwise.

An international recruiting agency in Melbourne told me this a couple of years ago: 'Our company had to recruit 6000 workers for a job in Asia. Twenty-four thousand people applied for those jobs. Nineteen-and-a-half per cent of them did not have their application even opened because we *did not like* their email address.'

Is this harsh or judgemental? It doesn't really matter. This is what is happening and it is something that can be easily be avoided.

What can you do?

Using your full name in your email address such as susanmclean@ is fine for adults, but for younger children, choose something that doesn't full identify them, such as smclean or s_mclean. These email addresses provide no information about the user such as their age or gender, which is very important in protecting children online. If you need to add a number, go for a random one; and steer clear of 69! Never add the year of birth, as this is a giveaway that the email account holder is a child, as are names such as cuddlybear, fluffycat and cookiemonster. Regardless of what you choose, go for sensible and respectful and don't try to be funny. It usually backfires.

Bluetooth phone names

Make sure you know your child's Bluetooth name and ensure that it is appropriate. Go into the settings on a Bluetooth-enabled device, open Bluetooth and search. It will locate all Bluetooth-enabled devices within range and the names will come up on your screen. Here is an example of some of the names I have found in schools around Australia:

- I'm a sexual predator
- I'm the local pedo
- I feel like killing someone today
- Luscious Lachlan (this turned out to be
  the deputy principal's phone – embarrassing)
- I'm 10 inches!
- Sexy Bitch
- Slutz phone.

Social media

Security settings

Although Facebook offers its users some excellent tools to keep information sharing to a minimum, and allows account holders to close their account to everyone except friends, the vast majority of users can't be bothered, don't know how, won't spend the time sorting it out or think they have their account settings private, only to find out later that they did not. Many other popular social networking sites such as Instagram and Kik offer limited security and privacy settings, so things posted on those sites are truly at the mercy of other users.

The reality is that privacy is not a concept that is remotely possible online. You can set security at different levels and you can limit who might see what, but that is all. You are relying on the fact that not *one* of your friends (or so-called friends) on Facebook will share your information with others. As nice as the idea of being able to trust your friends is, you can't always do so, as many people have discovered. Think of it this way: if your child has 650 friends on Facebook (most teens have around this number and many have substantially more) and they each had, say, 500 friends, then that is a total of 325000 people who could contact your child. The only word for that is dangerous.

Also worth noting is that Facebook has a different group of default security settings for account holders aged thirteen to seventeen years that are stricter than the default settings on an adult account. Set up your child's accounts correctly and use all the security that the site offers. If I looked up your child on a social networking site such as Facebook, the only things I should see are a name, a profile pic and a cover pic.

Security on Facebook

Help your teen protect their reputation on Facebook by following these steps:

- **Make the profile and cover pictures sensible.** No silly selfies, as you cannot look intelligent in them, or flirty beach pics. You can also use something non-identifiable such as your pet or sunset at the beach. This will be the first time someone gets to see you, so make it positive.

- **Check your child's friends.** After looking at the pics on your child's page, the next thing some people will do is look at all their friends, both real and otherwise, and form an opinion of your child based on what they can see in their friends' accounts.

- **Hide your child's friends from public view.** This stops others judging them on what their friends appear to be like: good or, more importantly, bad. Another reason for hiding their friends is to prevent people seeing that they have a friend in common and then gaining access to your child's account by contacting that person. This is morally wrong, but not illegal.

- **Protect the photos.** Photos on your child's page should be set so that only their friends can see them, never the public or friends of friends. But remember that nothing is truly private so you may find that embarrassing pic now cached and locatable in a Google image search.
- **Know how tagging works.** Make sure you manage the tagging option so that your child cannot be tagged in a potentially embarrassing or awkward situation and then have it all over the internet for everyone to see. If your child is going to allow themselves to be tagged, set it so they have to approve the tag first.
- **Check your child's 'likes'.** Make sure that all those things your child has 'liked' are actually things they are happy to be associated with. Unknown to many parents, there are pages on Facebook that contain dangerous, disrespectful and hurtful content. Most kids will 'like' anything that a friend 'likes', often without checking what it is they are actually associating with. Remember, if you have 'liked' it, you are telling the world that you agree 100 per cent with what is on the page. Parents should check their children's 'likes' regularly, talk to them about what things they are 'liking' and explain the consequences of being linked to certain pages.

Other social media accounts/apps

By the time we work out how to protect ourselves on one account, a new one will pop up. It would be impossible to list all the accounts here, and realistically, some may be gone before you read this book. As a rule of thumb, you will need to learn about each site on which your child has a presence. Even if it is a well-known site, don't assume that the security settings are what they should be. Many sites explode in popularity far too quickly for the administrators to begin to sort out what they *should* have thought of earlier. Many apps and sites actively encourage public settings or have a very limited ability to restrict access. Many don't scramble metadata, which means if your child's GPS settings are on and they post a pic, they can be easily located.

Google your child

Many of the things your child does online will be found quickly and easily by a simple Google search of their name. When you do a Google search, you don't actually search the web. You are searching Google's index of the web. The more your child uses technology, the more it will have stored about them. You will often find links to all their accounts, including ones they may have had when they were really young (read foolish) and accounts they have forgotten to close down. Blogs, postings, comments, school newsletters, sport club news, in fact everything involving your child is just a click away. Once it's there, it is very difficult to remove, even if you don't like it.

What if I find something I don't like?

Issues surrounding bullying, harassment, photos used without permission and so on can be dealt with by reporting it to legitimate sites. These sites will respond promptly and most often remove the content when requested. Others that have lax security settings and a don't-care attitude offer little or nothing in the way of assistance. Forewarned is forearmed and often the sooner you act, the better the outcome. If you are unhappy with something you've found, the best thing to do is contact the source or the site and ask for immediate removal.

The digital footprint management quick response checklist

- Choose email addresses and usernames sensibly. Consider what an email address says about your child.
- Set all accounts to the highest privacy setting.
- Only link to a reasonable number of people your child *actually* knows.
- Hide friends from public view.
- Hide other things like groups and likes.
- Untag/delete photos or videos that are inappropriate.
- Check that friends of friends cannot obtain information.
- Regularly check account settings to ensure ongoing security.
- Check and review account interactions: delete posts, comments and blog entries that have the potential to be taken the wrong way or could be perceived as negative.
- Regularly google your child and deal with anything that is damaging.
- Delete old or unused accounts. If your child is not actively using the account, get rid of it.
- Make sure that any voicemail on your child's phone has an appropriate tone.
- Don't be complacent – check, double-check and act promptly if the need arises.

CHAPTER 4

WHAT ARE CHILDREN DOING ONLINE?

Most of the issues that get reported to me tend to stem from a parent's lack of understanding of what a device is actually capable of, what their child is capable of doing with that device and what the actual risks in cyberspace are. Every digital device that has the ability to connect to the internet should be considered to be potentially dangerous. It really does not matter what the device is; the risks of connectivity are the same. Some devices are easier to manage than others. Large devices are easy to see and monitor, but smaller ones that can be secreted under a doona are almost impossible to monitor.

What devices are they using?

Nearly all electronic devices today will have some sort of connectivity. The following is a list of the most commonly used internet-enabled devices, to help you understand exactly what your child might be using and what conversations you need to have about the safe, respectful and responsible use of such device.

Computers

Desktop computers: A bit old-fashioned and very yesterday, the benefits of a desktop computer are that all the components are contained within the device.

Laptop computers or notebooks: This is a small portable computer in what is called a clamshell design, developed to allow for portability. A laptop has mostly the same components as a desktop, but as the devices have become smaller, some things like CD/DVD ROMs have to be attached externally. The mouse is contained in a touch or track pad and most have inbuilt speakers and a webcam.

Netbooks: Developed in late 2007 as a smaller, cheaper and lighter version of a laptop, they are now mostly superseded by tablets.

Ultrabooks: The new Ultrabook laptop is much lighter than a traditional laptop, but with the same processing capabilities. Due to their limited size, they typically omit common laptop features such as CD/DVD drives and ethernet ports.

Tablets

Apple: The most popular tablet today is the iPad. There have been five versions of the standard-size iPad since its launch, including the latest version known as the iPad Air. There have also been two versions of the iPad Mini, which was first launched in November 2012. The user interface is built around the device's multi-touch screen, including a virtual keyboard. The iPad also has built-in wi-fi and, on some models, cellular connectivity, meaning you can use a prepaid or post-paid data pack. An iPad can take pictures and videos, play music and games and search the web, and also supports email. One of the key features of the iPad is its ability to run a multitude of apps, including those for entertainment, socialising, and those that are considered educational.

Android: They say that imitation is the highest form of flattery, so once Apple launched the iPad, others were keen to follow. Samsung Galaxy Note, ASUS Transformer Pad and Fonepad, Microsoft Surface Pro and Google Nexus are examples of an Android tablet device. All are similar to the iPad but have different features such as the ability to use an S pen (stylus pen) or a keyboard dock, making them more like a mini laptop. Running on the Android operating system means that you get your apps from Google Play. A recent count on Google Play turned up 800000 different apps. If you wanted to see them all you would need to download 90 apps an hour for a year!

MP3 players

An MP3 player is a portable media player, most commonly used to listen to music but which can now support video and pictures. Stand-alone MP3 players have diminished in popularity as smart phones have the same technology integrated into their operating systems. The most popular MP3 player on the market today is the iPod Touch, which many parents purchase for their children instead of buying them a phone, thinking they will be much safer. Many also think that these devices are used solely to listen to music. Parents may be unaware until there is a problem that this device connects to the internet, and is able to download apps including those with messaging features such as Kik, and also VoIP programs such as Skype, so in reality it operates almost like a phone. These devices need to be kept out of the bedroom as well.

Mobile phones

Well, haven't mobile phones changed since their inception? Lovingly called a brick (because it was about the size of one), it originally did little other than make and receive very expensive phone calls. Motorola made the first handheld phone in 1973. It weighed 1.1 kg and was 23 cm long. It offered 30 minutes' talk time and took ten hours to recharge!

There are three types of mobile phone: Apple's iPhone, the Android (everything except iPhone and Nokia) and the Symbian (Nokia) phone. While the operating systems are different, the function of the phones themselves is pretty similar. While the iPhone was the forerunner when it came to touch-and-swipe screen technology, many other phones have this feature as well. Smart phones can do everything a laptop and tablet can do, plus of course make and receive phone calls. Other devices use the internet for voice calls. Phones and tablets also use apps; there are stand-alone apps and also app versions of websites that you may use on your desktop or laptop. Internet banking and social networking sites are two examples of having both systems in place. All of the games your child plays on a phone will be in app format.

Remember that phones today are called 'smart phones' for a reason. Sometimes it is better for parents to purchase what I call a 'dumb phone' for their child. They are still available and can be a useful option to consider. These phones do not do much more than send and receive calls and texts. They do not connect to the internet and some don't have a camera. If you chose to equip your child with a smart phone, be aware that almost all smart phones allow for restrictions that parents can set to limit what the phone can do, what your child can access and download and so on. Make sure you know how to use these controls before giving the device to your child (see page 133 for using parental controls and other tips). It will save you a lot of heartache in the future, guaranteed. To get started, have a look at these:

- For parental controls on an Android phone,
  visit the Google Play app store and download
  the app called Android Parent Control.
- For parental controls on an iPhone, there are inbuilt
  restrictions that you can install by going to settings,

general, restrictions, then installing a restrictions
passcode so that your child cannot change them back.
- For the Nokia phone, have a look at the following website:
http://handheld.softpedia.com.

Gaming consoles

The first (and very basic) consoles, Atari and Nintendo, led the way
with popular home gaming. Over the years many have come and gone.
Can you remember the Sega SG-1000 or the Commodore 64? Find a
picture of them online and show your kids. They really do look like
something out of the 'olden days', yet we are only talking around thirty
years ago.

The three main brands we currently associate with TV-connected
gaming consoles are the Nintendo Wii, the Sony PlayStation and the
Microsoft Xbox. The Nintendo and PlayStation also have smaller
handheld consoles. They all do similar things, and it really is a matter of personal preference, much like choosing a brand of motor car.
Some games are only released for one brand of console, and some people game on a specially configured computer with enhanced graphics.
Where and how you game is really up to you, but as a parent, what do
you need to know?

Nintendo Wii / Wii U: Nintendo released the Wii gaming console in 2006. Its key difference from other gaming consoles is the Wii
remote, which can be used as a handheld pointing device and which
detects movement in three dimensions. It has parental controls and
the ability to turn the internet off.

Sony PlayStation 4: The successor to the PlayStation 3, or PS3, it
can be fully integrated with other devices and operating systems as well
as connecting to the internet for online game playing.

PlayStation Vita: This is a handheld gaming console developed and marketed by Sony as the successor to the PlayStation Portable. It primarily competes with the Nintendo 3DS, as part of the eighth generation of gaming.

Xbox One: Microsoft's Xbox One is a video game console that is the successor to the Xbox 360 and is the third console in the Xbox family. It directly competes with Sony's PlayStation 4 and Nintendo's Wii U. It is considered to be an 'all-in-one entertainment system', making it a competitor to other home media devices such as the Apple TV and the Google TV platforms.

Nintendo 3DS/3DS XL: This small, portable handheld gaming device supersedes the Nintendo DS. It is capable of projecting stereoscopic 3D effects without the need for additional accessories or 3D glasses. It competes in the handheld game market with the Sony Vita.

What sites/apps are they using?

It's simply not good enough to have no idea! If you are going to let your child play a game or have an account on a site, then you *must* set up an account yourself *before* you allow your child to access the site, to see what level of interaction and contact is possible. The main danger young people face when using internet technology is not with the device at all; it is with what they are using it for. Children sometimes think they are anonymous online – and some apps even promise anonymity – which may lead them to send a nasty text or an inappropriate photo.

Of course, as a child grows and develops the risks and dangers change. As we are seeing younger and younger children online, we need to be aware of how best to protect our children at each age and stage of their development. There are too many sites, apps and games to list them all, but here are the main ones that I come across regularly – most especially when talking to parents and schools about what children are doing online. (See also page 123.) By obeying the age restrictions, enforcing security settings and encouraging proper usage, you can help prevent your child from many of the dangers that lurk online.

Site	Description	Age
Ask.fm and Qoohme	Social networking sites where users are encouraged to ask each other questions anonymously.	13+
Facebook	The biggest social networking site in the world. Comprehensive security settings with stricter defaults for teen account holders.	13+
FaceTime	Video chat application developed by Apple. Can connect with any of your contacts that use Apple devices.	13+
Instagram	A photo-sharing/social networking site now owned by Facebook. Although users can choose to share privately, most do not. GPS location of photos can be easily obtained if privacy settings are not enabled.	13+

Kik	An instant messaging app that is highly appealing to kids because it is free and you don't need a phone to use it – it works with the iPod touch. Communication is via any wi-fi network, so calls/texts do not come out of phone credit. Many schools I work with have mentioned this app because younger kids are using it without their parents' knowledge.	13+ but rated 17+
Snapchat	A photo messaging app that allows users to send a photo to another user that will dissolve off the screen in between one and ten seconds. Contrary to popular belief, the photos are **not** deleted, and users can take a screen shot of photos.	13+
Skype	VoIP program that allows users to make free voice and video calls over wi-fi network. It also allows text chat.	All ages
Tinder	An online dating app that connects people based on locality and interests. Popular with teens.	13+
Tumblr	Blogging site that allows you to post, comment and share your thoughts about anything of interest to you. You can also follow other users to see what they are posting.	13+

Twitter	Microblogging site where each tweet is limited to 140 characters or less. Very popular with high-profile people including sports stars and celebrities.	13+
YouTube	Video-sharing site. Monitor closely and use parental controls to limit exposure to age-inappropriate content.	13+ to have an account, any age to view

> After a mother found her eleven-year-old daughter had been chatting to dubious strangers online, she commented, 'The game looked so babyish compared to what is out there, and I had no idea you can interact within apps!'

Most of these apps and sites have easily recognisable logos. It's a good idea for parents to familiarise themselves with them so a quick glance at your child's screen will let you know what they are using.

Parenting in cyberspace must be about identifying and managing the risk and minimising the potential negative consequences. The best piece of advice I can give you is the Boy Scouts' motto 'Be prepared'. You cannot protect your children if you don't know what you need to protect them from. Children don't think like adults, they don't have life experiences and what for them is a bit of fun can quickly turn to a dangerous or hurtful experience if you're not on top of what's out there.

CHAPTER 5

WHEN AN ONLINE FRIEND IS NOT A FRIEND AT ALL

Who is your child's new online BFF (Best Friend Forever)?

Although the internet did not create child predators, it has significantly increased the opportunities child sex offenders have to meet victims while minimising the risk of detection. Why would a predator lurk at shopping malls, cinemas or sports grounds to ply their trade and risk being seen, when they can hide behind a veil of perceived anonymity online and connect with thousands of children every day? As technology has evolved, the street corner of the twenty-first century is now the internet and its plethora of social networking sites, apps and games.

This is not to say that those who abuse children don't hang out in the real world too, but the internet and mobile phone technology allow these people to ply their trade out of the glare of parents, carers, teachers and others entrusted to look after young people. Hiding behind the interface that is the internet and pretending to be whoever they want to be is extremely simple. As much as I hate using the word clever to describe online child predators, they are very good at what they do, and they rely on the fact that while kids know their way around technology, their cognitive development lags behind.

There are risks for all children who use the internet or online services. Teenagers are particularly at risk because they often use the computer unsupervised and are more likely than younger children to participate in online discussions about more personal issues such as sexual activity. Young people are naturally curious and will engage in online discussions about things that they would not openly discuss in the real world. They chat with strangers for fun, because 'everyone else is', and because they do not and cannot see the danger.

Online grooming

Most children actually believe and will tell you that they do not speak to 'pedos' (paedophiles) online, and that they could pick one out if contact was made. This sounds fine in theory, and often lulls parents into a false sense of security, but it is flawed in practice. Online predators do not send friend requests identifying themselves as paedophiles. Online predators take advantage of a child's natural vulnerabilities, such as their desire to appear adult, their need for attention, their wanting to please and not make people angry.

Grooming is the process by which these people connect with a child and develop a relationship. Online grooming is conducted in a similar fashion to grooming in the real world and is often a preliminary step to procuring, where the adult attempts to loosen the child's inhibitions regarding sexual activity or heighten their curiosity by sending pornographic material or talking about sexual matters. The predator's aim is to eventually meet the child in person for the purposes of sexual activity. The process often includes sending the child pornographic images so as to normalise the requests, and then moves to asking the child to send naked images of themselves or perform a sex act on a webcam.

Online grooming starts with sending communication, messages and comments to the child to elicit a sense of friendship and trust. Online predators trawl social media sites and post hundreds of complimentary comments such as, 'Saw your pic and you look hot', or, 'You have nice eyes', or, 'I bet you're prettier IRL [In real life]', and, 'You're so sexy', which target the insecurities most adolescents feel about their bodies, and of course these comments make them feel good about themselves. They think, this person must be nice as they are sending me compliments and being kind to me. Everyone likes to be complimented and have people like them; it is natural and predators know this. They also know that if you are nice to someone, they will most likely be nice back.

This process does not happen overnight and predators are persistent if they get a child to engage with them. After the compliments often come gifts, mobile phone credit, iTunes gift cards, mobile phones and devices that allow even easier and continual contact. No young person is ever going to say no to more phone credit or a new phone! Their goal is to make their potential victim feel loved and comfortable, to become the most important person in the child's life and as such have a degree of control over them. They will empathise with them and sympathise: 'I know how that feels, it happened to me', 'I had a crappy day too, my mum yelled at me and just doesn't get it either'. They will be up-to-date on popular music, films, movies, and online games.

As the grooming process continues, so too does the level of trust and the strength of the relationship. The victim will share more and more personal and private information. They will share hopes and dreams, secrets and private information and in many cases, a child will even provide the online predator with the passwords to their accounts. For kids, passwords are a commodity that they will willingly share to prove their friendship. Once an online predator has a child's password and access to their accounts, they will without a doubt be able to find something to hold over them, a comment about being drunk, a racy pic, a party they attended when they shouldn't have.

Once they have gained their victim's trust, they will slowly start introducing sexual content to their conversations to lower the child's inhibitions. This may start simply with a request for a 'sexy pic' or a question such as, 'Are you horny?' Initially the response will be no, but because of the level of control these people have over their victims, and the fact that they are very persistent, it is often just a matter of time. Comments such as, 'If you like me you would send one', or, 'Prove to me how much you like me', play on the child's emotions. Often they may send the child pornography or naked pics to normalise the request: 'See, everyone is doing it, it's fine', or, 'Now you have a pic of me, you need to send one back'. Another method used to convince a victim to participate is to threaten to tell about something embarrassing. Remember this predator has been provided with lots of personal information during the grooming process, so has the ability to blackmail the child into doing what is asked of them.

Just a few weeks ago, I visited a school for student sessions during the day and a parent seminar at night. I had finished the Year 7 session and was waiting for the next session to start when one of the students, a 12-year-old boy, asked if he could speak to me. 'Of course,' I said, and instantly the young student's voice began to crack and he became very upset. I moved him into a private area and asked him to take a deep breath and tell me what was bothering him.

He told me he had been playing the game World of Warcraft (MA15+) and had connected with another player, an adult male. This person seemed nice, was interested in the game and offered to play with the boy every week. This was very appealing to the young student and over time a level of trust was gained by the older man. The man asked the boy if he was on Skype and would he like to chat. The boy saw nothing wrong with chatting to his new gaming friend and initially things were fine. Then the man asked for photos as well as chatting on Skype via the webcam. He told the boy that 'he had no children any more', and that made him sad. He also said the only time he felt happy was when he could see this young boy. He was playing on the vulnerability of this young boy and the fact that the young boy wanted to make his new friend happy. He then asked for the boy to take his clothes off and perform certain acts on the webcam. He told the young boy that he would not keep playing unless he took his clothes off. He also told the young boy he loved him and the only time he felt happy was when he was watching him naked online. Sadly the boy obliged. He said to me that he did not want to 'upset' his online friend. The man was also often naked.

I asked him if the man had suggested they meet. He got very upset and said that they were meant to meet last weekend but he had lied to the man, saying he couldn't come because he had to help his mother. Telling this lie was almost as upsetting for this young boy as what had happened to him and illustrates just how vulnerable children are. I asked him if his parents were aware of what was going on and he said no. He did say that his mother had noticed him crying on the weekend and asked what was wrong. He replied that someone was being mean to him online. The mother did not investigate further or probe what was actually happening and, concerningly, he told me his parents didn't think it was necessary to attend the parent session that evening!

How do these people find your child?

Online predators work on what I call the 'burglar' concept. A person wanting to break in and steal from your house doesn't usually want *your* house; they want any house that might have something of value in it to steal, and they will go down a street looking at each house to see which would be the easiest and quickest to break into. They will bypass houses with good security, barking dogs, alarms and deadlocks, and just keep going until they hit the jackpot, so to speak. A house with no security, perhaps a window left open, and bingo – success. The same thing applies online.

These predators trawl the streets of cyberspace just looking for someone – anyone – to connect with so they can start the grooming process. Sites and accounts with high security will be overlooked for the child whose account is available to everyone online. The child that immediately blocks a friend request from someone they don't know, or does not engage with someone they don't really know, will be overlooked for the child who doesn't do these things. Online predators are moving their business into apps as they know there are often limited security settings available and also that younger and younger children are using them – on phones, on the iPod Touch, and in bedrooms out of sight of parents.

The fact that most children now have access to portable and easily hidden mobile devices means that they are providing online predators with an ease of access that they have never experienced before. Just as easily as an adult finds another adult online, predators find kids. They know the popular sites that kids use, such as:

- Kik
- Instagram
- Facebook
- Snapchat

- Skype
- Tumblr
- You Tube.

They know the ones that have limited security settings, the ones that are app-based, and the ones younger kids use on tablets and iPods. They also know the games kids play, and they play them too. They set up accounts on social networking sites and trawl until they find someone willing to chat.

Some of these sites and apps have relatively good safety settings and others don't, but you cannot rely on the site to keep your child safe. It is up to the individual users and, for young children, parental supervision is of course vital.

Smart devices include built-in geolocation technologies that allow you to identify the physical location of the device. This can give other people using the same applications as your child real-time access to their location. Quite simply, they can find out where you live. You need to know which apps on your child's device use location services, and how to disable them.

Follow these steps to turn off location services on an Apple device:

> Settings
> Privacy
> Location services (either turn it all off, or
  leave it on and turn off individual ones from
  the list of apps you use, such as the camera).

For Android devices and other non-iOS systems, do the following:

> Settings
> Location or something similar, depending on the device
> Off (either turn it all off, or turn it off for individual apps
  such as the camera).

A Year 7 girl posted a picture of herself on her public Instagram account. A few minutes later she had a reply: 'Nice house you live in at . . .' with her address and a Google Street View picture of her house attached.

Someone had taken the posted picture, read the metadata (location services were 'on') and got the location. Scary.

Why don't kids listen when the alarm bells sound?

Everyone has instincts, a way of behaving, thinking or feeling that is not learned. There are also early warning signs, specific physical indicators that alert us to possible risks to our safety. Examples can be a racing heart, getting the shakes or clammy hands, in fact anything that your body does to tell you that something is not right. A young child's instincts are developing along with their bodies, each child at a different rate. Young children simply do not have the confidence and maturity to trust their instincts and acknowledge the early warning signs, and remove themselves from a situation. Even adolescents, who on reflection could identify the warning signs of impending danger, often do not have the ability to act on them and remove themselves from that danger.

The following are three recent actual cases where the dangers will appear obvious to an adult, and were identified by the young person, but not acted upon. The young people involved are not to be viewed as silly; the examples illustrate in different ways just how clever online predators are and how (despite feeling uncomfortable and thinking things are a bit strange) kids just don't act on the warning signs the way an adult would.

Example 1

It was early in the year and a fifteen-year-old boy – we will call him Tom – had recently changed secondary schools so most of his mates were from his previous school, with just a few at his current school. Tom was chatting to a mate from his old school (let's call him Ben) on Facebook and Ben said to Tom, 'You should add "Jane Doe" as a friend, she is awesome.' Ben asked Tom who this girl was and Ben replied that he had no idea but 'she will send you naked pics of herself anytime you ask! All my mates have her as a friend'. Tom immediately added 'Jane' and, true to her word, she started to send naked pics of herself. This went on a for a few weeks, and after a while, some of the comments from 'Jane' seemed a bit weird, but hey, if you're onto a good thing, stick to it, right? So Tom kept up the communication and it got more and more sexual in nature. 'Jane' then asked Tom for a few pics of himself in return. He was pretty happy with himself, and flattered that such a hot girl like Jane wanted his pics, so he sent some naked ones back.

This continued for a while, with Tom occasionally feeling like something was a bit off but not enough to stop or tell anyone. Then came demands for specific types of pics. Tom obliged, although feeling uncomfortable. After attending a presentation I gave at his school, he went home and told his mother what was going on as he started to think it might not be okay. All the little niggling issues that he had chosen to overlook now seemed worrying and real. His mother rang seeking advice and when I looked up the account belonging to 'Jane Doe' it was pretty clear that something was not right. Several things jumped out at me:

- The profile had a very Western name but an image of a dark-skinned Asian or Indian female as the profile pic.

- Most of the friends on the account were young white males, with some young Asian-looking girls as well.
- The pics on the account were of a variety of different young girls (with subtle differences, but no faces visible).
- All the comments posted to the timeline were of a highly sexual nature.

Tom's mother also said Tom told her that on reflection, the naked pics that 'Jane' had sent now appeared to be of several different girls with some very subtle differences, things that on first glance you would not notice: freckles, piercings and skin tone. It also appeared that a few of Tom's friends had felt it was strange enough to block 'Jane'. Tom was also worried about the naked pics he had sent, which at the time had seemed like a good idea.

They placed the issue in the hands of the police and an investigation was started that substantiated Tom's concerns. He was being groomed. Tom was a good kid: smart, sporty, well behaved, academic and with great family support, yet he'd been tricked. He had not trusted his instincts and chose to ignore the little niggles, the warning signs, but such is the hold these people can have on their victims. They are clever and calculating and use a variety of methods to illicit what they want.

Example 2

A school teacher set up a fake account on Facebook, pretending to be a talented surfer from the Margaret River region of Western Australia. The teacher then told his students that he had heard there was a new student coming to the school, and when the girls got Facebook friend requests from this fake account, they *assumed* it was the new student and added him. It really is not that hard to get kids to add people as friends to their Facebook account anyway, but by planting the notion of a new student, the predator made it seem safe.

One victim, who was fourteen at the time, said that she relented and sent the boy pictures of herself because he 'begged' her every day. This tactic is common: badger them until they give in. Often kids simply relent and send the pic in the misguided belief that this will 'get rid' of the problem. She also said, 'He wanted me to say dirty things. It felt awkward, uncomfortable and weird. It kind of felt like I needed to or he would get mad.' Clearly the young victim was upset by what was happening, but the desire to please and be liked won out over her ability to put her own feelings first. She also said that he would send pictures of his penis and in return she would send back naked ones of herself: 'You have one of me so I need one of you'. Later she said, 'He would talk really grown up for a fourteen year old. He would use the word beautiful instead of hot or sexy, which boys that age would. He wrote sentences very properly.' Again, something was not right. This girl also found the boy's pics on another website unrelated to the boy and his name.

Another victim told the court that she received a friend request from the boy and accepted because he had fifteen other mutual friends, all girls from the same town. This is just so common. Once online predators have gathered a couple of friends, then they simply target those people's friends until no-one questions who they are. The second victim also said, 'The first thing he said to me was I had beautiful eyes.' A week later he asked for photos. He kept asking and eventually she gave in.

The man was found guilty and jailed for three years.

Example 3

A mother of two teenage boys rang me for advice. They lived in a very remote mining town with a small permanent population but a large population of FIFO (Fly In, Fly Out) workers. Earlier that evening, one of her sons had confided in her that he was very worried that a young 'girl' who was his friend on Facebook was not all she seemed. This young girl was Facebook friends with all the young males in town and had an attractive profile and cover picture. She stated she was eighteen years old and listed her former secondary school, a well-known school in the capital city, as well as her current location, which was a different mining town. As this girl was Facebook friends with all the young boys, it was assumed that someone must actually know her.

She had developed what could be called a relationship with one of the mother's two boys and over time, naked pictures were exchanged. First she sent some of herself and insisted on some in return. The boy obliged and then the girl started to make suggestions as to the pose she wanted in the picture. She also asked the boy to shave his pubic hair and then send some more. It was at this point that the boy began to have doubts about who he was dealing with. Using the geolocation information, he identified that the person was not in another mining town, but located at the local caravan park.

Not knowing what to do, the mother rang Crime Stoppers and also got in touch with me. I made contact with the listed school to check out the so-called former student, who of course did not exist. I then reported it to the Online Child Exploitation Squad and one month later the mother rang to say that an arrest had been made.

These three examples show how predators can work and how young people often don't have the level of maturity or development to take notice of the warning signs and act on them. This is exactly why adults need to understand their methods, how they ply their trade and how best to protect the children in their care. As UK Crown Prosecutor Andrew McFarlane, when prosecuting the case of defendant Michael Williams, the UK's worst ever online child sex offender, stated:

Ironically, in this day and age, many parents don't let
their children out at night lest they meet someone like the
defendant. Instead, they feel they are safe in their bedroom
but unknown to the parents, some children were meeting the
defendant using their computers. It is a chilling reflection.

What are the alarm bells?

Here are some signs to look out for in your children that may suggest something is wrong:

- Your child spends more time than normal, and longer periods of time, online.
- They receive phone calls and texts more frequently and want to deal with them away from their parents.
- They receive physical gifts from people *you* don't know.
- You find pornography or sexually explicit images on your child's device. (Paedophiles will often send pornographic images in order to 'normalise' their requests for pictures.)
- There are people on your child's 'friends' list that they don't really know.
- They never seem to run out of phone credit, when they did previously.

- They become withdrawn and secretive, and their demeanour changes for the worse.

If you are at all concerned about the possibility of your child being a victim of online grooming, please contact your local police station for advice and assistance.
If you believe that your child or another child is in immediate danger, phone 000 or your local law enforcement emergency phone number.

Protecting your child online – quick response checklist

- Be involved in everything that your child does online. This is your responsibility as a parent.
- Take an interest in what they do online and who they communicate with, just as you would in the real world.
- Talk to them, constantly. Cybersafety is an ongoing issue and the conversations must continue and evolve as required.
- Make sure that all internet access occurs in a common or public area of the house and regularly check the screen.
- Set realistic time limits for online interactions, never unsupervised (for younger children) and never in bedrooms when you are asleep at night or at work. (See Chapter 10 for more online safety tips.)
- Teach them about the methods online predators use and ensure that they know they can come to you regardless of what has happened.
- Teach your children not to have conversations about sex with people they have met online. Make sure they know to tell you if this happens.
- Teach them about why you don't share identifying information – names, phone numbers and schools – and about geotagging of photos.
- Continue educating yourself and remember to trust your instincts. If you feel that something is not right, then it probably isn't.

CHAPTER 6

CYBERBULLYING: THE SURVIVAL GUIDE

Managing any issue that is having a negative impact on your family is stressful, especially one that you don't really understand or have little experience in dealing with, and one that may seem outside your control. While schools quickly and successfully resolve most instances of cyberbullying among students, there are always exceptions. Regardless of how quickly action is taken, it is still a very distressing and hurtful experience for all involved, especially children. As a parent you may also have to deal with the fact that it is your child who has behaved inappropriately online. A lot of times this is simply because the child is not mature enough to understand the consequences of their actions. People say things online that they would never say in the real world. Kids often copy what others do or believe their comment was made in 'fun'. Sometimes, of course, kids will intentionally behave in a hurtful way, but this is not the norm. This chapter is designed to help you deal with cyberbullying in its many forms and with its many consequences.

What is cyberbullying?

Cyberbullying is a way of delivering covert psychological bullying:
> *It uses information and communication technologies*
> *to support deliberate, repeated, and hostile behaviour by*
> *an individual or group, that is intended to harm others.*
> (Bill Belsey 2007)

Cyberbullying can be described as any repeated harassment, insults or humiliation that occur through electronic mediums such as email, mobile phones, social networking sites, instant messaging programs, chat rooms, websites and online games. Cyberbullying usually occurs between people who are known to each other, such as students at a school, members of a sporting club, someone from your social circle or a friend of a friend; at the very least, it's usually someone you know of. Cyberbullies do not normally drop from cyberspace and attach themselves to your child.

Cyberbullying is different from a situation when we see an individual attacked online by a large number of different people. This is often called trolling. In these cases, there is often no direct connection between parties other than a desire to hurt another person. The actions of the troll can be described as intentionally provocative and harassing.

Cyberbullying is pervasive in nature, incessant, ongoing, and can occur 24/7. It is different from bullying in the real world as by virtue of technology the bully can follow you home and into your house. It often occurs with the perception of anonymity, such as with an account in a fake name or a blocked number, but in many cases it is clear who is behind the bullying. Like any form of bullying, cyberbullying can be psychologically damaging, which is often more difficult for parents to identify and subsequently act upon. It is far harder to see mental anguish than a bruise on a leg, so be aware of any subtle changes in your child's demeanour or behaviour and investigate accordingly. Cyberbullying is also very public humiliation, as many others see what is written or posted, and once a message or comment is posted online, even if the perpetrator deletes it, it is almost impossible to remove all traces of the message.

Children will often re-read the comment over and over, which further upsets them. Adults have the maturity to know it's better not to do this. This is one of the reasons that cyberbullying is particularly hurtful to young people, who do not have cognitive maturity and life experiences to balance out the behaviour.

Examples of cyberbullying

Cyberbullying can include, but is not limited to:

- harassing and threatening messages sent using any form of technology
- sending nasty text messages, IMs (instant message, such as through Kik or Facebook Chat), MMS (picture messages) or repeated prank phone calls
- using a person's screen name to pretend to be them (setting up a fake account)
- using a person's password to access their account and then pretend to be them
- forwarding someone's private emails, messages, pictures or videos without permission
- posting mean or nasty comments or pictures
- sending sexually explicit images – 'sexting'
- intentionally excluding others from an online group.

Imagine your ten-year-old child comes to you, clearly upset, and tells you that some other kids are being mean and making fun of them online. Apparently your child posted a photo of a friend on Instagram as a joke, but the friend has taken it the wrong way and now everyone has ganged up against your child and are saying really hurtful things. You have a look at the comments and cannot believe what you are reading. The language is appalling and your child is clearly being targeted by many students. You were not even aware that your child had an Instagram account. What do you do?

- Stay calm.
- Support your child – let them know you will help.
- Praise them for coming to you.
- Resist retaliating or contacting other parents.
- Keep copies of everything.
- Notify your child's teacher as soon as possible (the next school day if you can) and provide evidence of what has happened. Leave it up to the school* to deal with it. They must also support your child.
- Explain your disappointment at your child creating an account on a site without your permission and also against the age restrictions.
- Discuss with your child the problem with 'joking' online, and how easy it is to be taken the wrong way. Explain that they made a poor decision, but what the other children did was wrong as well.
- Have a consequence that is relative to what has happened (delete the Instagram account and reduce technology time for a week).
- Seek professional assistance if required from a psychologist or counsellor.

- Use the situation as the basis for further conversations about online behaviour and your expectations. Revisit or establish an online safety family agreement (see page 141).

* Schools have a legal obligation to deal with all issues of cyberbullying and must do so. If you are not happy with the school's response, or if the school has done everything they can and it continues, then you can report it to police or the regional office of the relevant education body.

What do I look out for?

Trying to work out what is upsetting your child is often difficult. Teens can be moody, sullen, uninterested, joyous, loving and calm inter-changeably on a daily basis! It can be particularly hard to identify the cause as we need to consider illness, friendship issues, lower-than-expected grades at school, puberty and everything in between. However, we must be aware that the problem may be technology related.

Here is an edited letter I received from a mother (with identifying information changed):

Over the past month we have discovered that our son, 15, has been bullied, including over the internet. If I hadn't checked his Facebook messages, we would never have known. We noticed some changes in him mid 2013. The once popular funny, charismatic, smart kid became withdrawn, grades dropped etc, the same pattern as I'm sure you have heard before. Worried, I spoke to the school, who said he was doing well and is displaying typical teen behaviour. In November last year he was at an all-time low, saying everyone hated him and he is no good at anything. I decided to investigate and found these messages. They were awful, even saying he had had sex with me (his mum). I was gobsmacked and my husband was irate. "Max" no longer feels safe at his school so we have moved him and we have only just informed [his former school] about the Facebook messages, for which they are in the early stages of organizing discipline.

If I hadn't been to your presentation I may not have thought to check his Facebook page. My son is happy so far but worried about repercussions. The school is devastated they lost a kid like him. I am concerned of the effect it has had on him, despite his positive outlook. My husband wants to press charges.

How do we get through to kids that this is so serious? What they are doing pushes people over the edge. He was taunted with faggot, gay, try hard, everybody hates you. It leaves me so sad as a parent and equally concerned for my other children.

I said to my husband, I feel like we dodged a bullet. If we had not ... known, our son could possibly be another suicide statistic, and it would be too late. He told me once he'd rather die than go back to his former school. You can imagine that made me sit up and listen.

There is no definitive list of signs that could indicate cyberbullying, but the following are those known to be most common. You will note that the mother who wrote the letter above noticed many of these:

- **Change in mood and/or behaviour:** Most adolescents exhibit angry, upset or rebellious behaviours sometimes (some more than others). It is a normal and unavoidable part of growing up when hormones seem to take over and your child changes before your eyes. It is difficult to differentiate between normal adolescent angst and something more sinister, but trust your instincts and if you're concerned then investigate to try to get to the bottom of the problem. Regardless of the cause, if you don't know, you can't help.

- **Lower grades at school:** Any sudden downward change in your child's academic marks should be investigated. Often children who are being bullied show a distinct change in application to study and a lowering of marks.

- **Not wanting to go to school/sport, etc.:** Not wanting to be at the same place as the bully is normal. Going from having no issues heading out the door to school or sport to not wanting to go is a sure sign that something is not right. This can often manifest itself as random and non-specific 'ailments' that occur primarily just before having to leave for school or sport. Things such as headaches, stomach-aches or generally feeling sick may indicate an issue other than a medical illness.

- **Being extra secretive in online activities:** Kids often feel that they should have privacy when online and using a mobile phone. Be alert to secretive behaviours such as finding them online under the doona or in a 'secluded' part of the house, or always hiding the device when you are around, as a sign that something is going on.

- **Distinct change in online behaviours:** Take note of changes in your child's online behaviour. Examples include being jumpy when text messages arrive, not putting their phone down, wanting to be online all the time or never wanting to be online.

- **Change in friendship groups:** This may be no more than the normal change in friendships that will occur many times during your child's school days. If you are concerned, act on your worries and at least speak to your child's teacher. They are often aware of these things way before you as they get to see the class dynamics in action every day.

- **Spending more time with family instead of friends:** While it may seem nice that your child suddenly wants to hang out with you more than their friends, adolescence is a time where friends become *more* important and parents *less* so. Just be aware that things may not be okay in their world and be there for them. Ask if they are okay, or whether something has happened that is bothering them. Do they want to talk? Let them know you are there for them regardless. If you are still concerned, enlist the help of others. Getting help is not a sign of failure. People who can help you include your GP, school welfare staff, adolescent psychologist or family counsellor.

What do I do if my child is being bullied?

Do not be angry with your child: Remember they are the victim and it is someone else doing the wrong thing. *Do not* threaten to take technology away from them because of what someone else has done. This is one of the biggest barriers to kids telling their parents about online issues. Studies have shown that kids would rather put up with the negative rather than lose their online access.

1. Praise them for coming to you: This is a big step as most children are frightened to tell a parent about cyberbullying. Even if you don't really understand, let them know that you will help them. Try to stay as calm as possible.

You are the parent of a sixteen-year-old girl who attends the local high school. Most of her friends from primary school moved with her and she has also made some new friends. She is responsible, rarely gets into trouble and works hard at her studies. Like most teens, she loves technology and seems to never put her mobile down. You don't have too many concerns about her online activities as you feel she is a sensible girl, as are her friends. Unbeknown to you, your daughter has become a target for some of the other girls, and she is being cyberbullied on Facebook and Kik and via text. Over a period of a few weeks, her moods have changed, she is irritable and withdrawn, and she is jumpy when text messages arrive. She is clearly not herself. You also notice she is not online as much and when you ask about Facebook she says she is 'over it', and that her friends are so immature she can't be bothered with them either. You are particularly worried, so what should you do?

- Pick a suitable quiet time to raise your worries.
- Do not be alarmist, judgemental or angry.
- Calmly explain why you are worried and ask what is bothering her.
- **If she tells you,** you will need to find out: what has happened? Who is involved? Where has this occurred? Does she have copies? What has she done to try to stop it? Who has she told? What can you do now to assist? Ask her what she would like you to do.
- **If she refuses to tell you,** probe gently. Explain that it is a parent's job to worry, and there is nothing so bad that you can't talk about it together, that you will help no matter what. Seek out a trusted friend or sibling to see if they can get to the bottom of what is troubling your daughter. Persevere.

2. Save and store the content: Keep copies of the emails, chat logs or SMSs, comments or posts. Take a screen shot, cut and paste it to a Word document, whatever is easier for you. Don't worry if you do not know how to do this as most children know how to take screen shots. A couple of easy, non-technical ways to get hard copies are to bring the content up on the screen of a mobile phone, place the phone on a copy machine and press copy, or simply use another device to take a picture of the comment.

3. Help your child to block and delete the bully from all contact lists: Most reputable sites allow the user to control who can access them. Sit together to support your child as they do this. Many children feel 'mean' blocking another person, even if that person has already been mean to them, so support them and let them know that this is the correct thing to do. Explain that they should be in control of all their accounts and that if people behave in a way that is not respectful towards them they should be blocked (on some sites it is called 'ignore').

4. Do not respond: It is important not to respond to nasty emails, chats, SMS or comments; this is what the bully wants, so ignore them. Children will need your help and support to do this as it is natural to want to fight back. A short response such as, 'Stop this', is acceptable, but if your child responds with a threat or other unsuitable comment, then they may get themselves into trouble as well.

5. Use the 'report abuse' button: All reputable social networking sites, chat rooms, instant messaging programs and online games have a method by which you can let the site know that a particular person/account is behaving unacceptably or bothering you. Tell them the problems you are having and they are obligated to investigate.

Accounts can be deleted and warnings sent when users disobey the rules of the site. Some sites make this process easy; others are very complicated. It can be frustrating when you can't quickly find a way to report online abuse so sit and support your child while they do this.

6. Inform your child's school: It is important that they know what is going on so they can help and support your child and monitor any issues that may spill into the playground or classroom. If the bully is a fellow student, the school will assist you to work through the situation and deal with it as they would with any other bullying behaviours reported to them. If the bully is not from the same school, still ensure that the class teacher is aware so that they can also support your child in the same way as they would when any student has a problem. The same advice applies to sporting clubs, youth groups or workplaces. These organisations all have obligations in relation to dealing with inappropriate online interactions and must act.

7. Ensure they have some 'down time' without technology: It is important that your child's life is balanced so making sure that they are not online or spending hours on a mobile phone is important for both their mental and physical health (do not do this as punishment; rather as some peaceful time during which they are not being bothered). Set rules and boundaries around time spent online. Growing children need ten hours' sleep per night and teens between eight-and-a-quarter and nine-and-a-quarter hours per night. Phones and other devices that connect to the internet *should not* be in bedrooms, especially at night. The exception is if the wireless is turned off, but beware the child who can connect to the neighbour's unsecured network! Head to the closest discount department store and purchase a clock radio to defeat the cry of, 'But it's my alarm!'

8. Get a new phone number: As inconvenient as it is, this may be the best option if your child is being harassed via mobile phone. Some phone technology at the moment does allow for individual numbers to be blocked in the same way that online applications do but you cannot block a silent number. There are, however, programs that can be added to a mobile phone that will allow parents to set restrictions on the phone's use. Check with your mobile phone provider. You must also report the abuse to the phone company, who are obligated to investigate. Phone numbers can be changed at no cost if the request for a new number is as a result of ongoing abuse.

9. If unwanted contact continues: In most cases with prompt intervention, cyberbullying is successfully resolved. If, however, this is not the case, you may consider deleting current accounts and starting a new account, and tell your child to only give their new details to a small list of trusted friends.

10. If still ongoing, report it to police: Most school-based cyberbullying is satisfactorily resolved at school level, but there are always exceptions to the rule. Schools cannot report cyberbullying between individual students to the police so it is up to the victim (and parent) to make the report. A police report should not take the place of a school investigation, but you should do it if the school has tried and failed to stop the bullying. Police should always be informed about cyberbullying when:

- despite the best efforts of the school, it does not stop
- you have no idea who is behind the abuse (they are using fake accounts or blocked numbers)
- threats have been made to your child's personal safety.

Each state/territory has laws that prohibit online bullying, stalking and threatening behaviour (see Chapter 10). You don't have to put up with it.

What do I do if my child is the bully?

While it often comes as a shock to be told that your child has been bullying another student online, it is important that parents support the school in its handling of the situation. Don't try to lessen the issue or excuse your child's behaviour. As much as we want to protect our children, it is important that they learn inappropriate behaviour will come with a consequence. Schools have the expertise to deal with all parties to bullying behaviour and are legally obligated to do so. All schools have policies and programs to deal with students who bully others. Some use measures such as restorative justice or similar programs to support not only the victim but the bully as well.

As a parent, you have a major role to play to ensure that your child does not become or remain a bully. Be involved and aware of what your child is doing online, where they are going and who they are hanging out with. As difficult as it can be, children should be supervised when using technology and this is *your* responsibility as a parent. If you see comments they have made that are unpleasant, hurtful or nasty, speak to your child and explain why they should not behave this way online. Be vigilant and be involved. Parents have the ability to prevent the vast majority of online bullying.

Once you are aware that your child has bullied someone else online, you can support your child in these ways:

- Help them understand that their behaviour is unacceptable and possibly criminal as well. Also discuss why it is not okay to be mean online.
- Acknowledge that they may be feeling awful too;

they may be upset that they have done the wrong
thing, but let them see there are consequences.
Don't bail them out.

- Talk to them about their actions and try to find out
why they behaved in this way.
- Ask them to imagine how would they feel if they
were the victim (encourage empathy).
- Work together to improve the situation, such as
apologising.
- Support the school in their actions.
- Work towards preventing further incidents.
Set clear rules and boundaries about their online
behaviour and your expectations. Be vigilant and
be involved.
- Enlist the help of the school, welfare staff,
your local GP or a child psychologist.

Whether your child is being bullied or is the one doing the bullying,
stay calm, take a deep breath and try to be rational. It's easier said than
done and all parents feel considerable pain when their children are
hurt or upset. Often the parent is more upset than the child, and kids
are very resilient.

Never directly approach another child or their parents about a
bullying issue. Make an appointment with the school or the relevant
organisation, and take all of your supporting documents with you. Let
the school deal with it, but ensure that they have processes in place to
keep you up-to-date with what they are doing. Remember, they are
the experts in these things and need to be supported in order to resolve
these issues quickly and successfully. I have often seen cases where the
school has acted superbly and the kids have moved on, but the parents

want revenge and continue to make an issue out of the situation. Be guided by your children. If they're happy with the outcome, then be happy too. If not, take the matter further. By this I mean higher up at school, such as speaking to the principal, regional office or other relevant body. No-one has to put up with bullying or inaction, but please remember to be reasonable.

Cyberbullying quick-response checklist

- Don't respond.
- Block and delete the bully.
- Report the bullying to the site.
- Keep a copy of the abusive comments.
- Tell the school (or relevant place) and seek action.
- If the bullying is ongoing, inform the police.
- Support your child.

CHAPTER 7

SEXTS AND SELFIES: WHAT WILL THEY THINK OF NEXT?

The very thought that one of your children would even consider taking a naked picture of themselves is enough to make any parent sick in the stomach. Then add the thought that this picture has not only been taken, but sent off into cyberspace, to remain there forever, and the feeling is nothing short of horror.

One thing that my experience in dealing with these issues over many years has taught me is that the child who sends a sext is often the child deemed least likely. So often it's the kid who normally makes good decisions, is well behaved and never in trouble at school. This can come like a bolt out of the blue for parents and teachers. I can't tell you how many times I've had phone calls from very distressed mums and dads, with them saying, 'I never would have believed they would do this', or, 'She/he is only eleven'.

Most parents feel abject failures at this point, and believe it is all their fault. Although a normal reaction, it isn't helpful to beat yourself up over this. It is important to understand that for many kids, the decision to take and send a naked selfie is instantaneous and something that in some cases cannot be prevented. You can do your best, but at some point your child will make a decision that will have a negative impact. This is very much one of these situations.

The alarming thing is that taking and sending naked selfies is not just confined to adolescents. Some kids in primary school are doing it too. I don't think anyone has the answer to 'Why do they do it?' but we need to understand what we are talking about, how and when it can happen, and what to do afterwards.

What is sexting?

Sexting – sending a sexy text – or the newer term naked selfie, is the act of sending sexually explicit messages, photos or videos electronically, primarily between mobile phones, but it can be done via internet apps such as Instagram, Snapchat or Kik, or via social networking sites. Other names for these pictures include noodz, banana pic, tit pic and its reciprocal, the rather crude dick pic.

Children today are exposed to a wide range of sexual imagery, in the words of songs, video clips, movies, the internet and advertising. Many young pop stars exude sex and sexuality, which can cause impressionable and vulnerable young people to form the opinion that this behaviour is mainstream and totally acceptable. The reality is of course the opposite and children often only become aware of this after the event.

A mother spoke to me recently about the following dilemma. Her thirteen-year-old daughter had come to her and showed her a pic posted on the Instagram account of a close friend, also thirteen. It was from the neck down, and the young girl was wearing very skimpy underwear and the pose was highly sexual. The attached comment was, 'I finally f***en love my body and I don't care what you c**** think!'

The mother didn't know what to do. She discussed the picture and comments with her daughter, who was equally horrified and said that she thought her friend was stupid to post such a picture. She was also worried about her and where the picture would end up. The girls now attended different high schools but the mother was still close to the other mother. Should she contact her?

I suggested she meet with the mother for coffee and gently tell her what had happened. No accusations, just show her the pic and comments and say, 'I know this is upsetting, but if this was my daughter I would hope someone would let me know.' Take her lead and show support. Don't argue but walk away if things become tense. You have done the right thing.

If you don't know the other parent, my advice is to tell the school principal of the child involved. They will absolutely thank you.

The Pew Internet Project and the University of Michigan (2009) conducted six focus groups with middle- and high-school students in three cities as part of a wider study. In this study teens described the pressure they felt to share these types of images. One high school girl wrote:

When I was about 14–15 years old, I received/sent these types
of pictures. Boys usually ask for them or started that type of
conversation. My boyfriend, or someone I really liked asked
for them and I felt like if I didn't do it, they wouldn't continue
to talk to me. At the time, it was no big deal but now looking
back it was definitely inappropriate and over the line.

The issue of these naked pics usually falls into one of three broad categories:

1. Young people wanting to impress a potential boyfriend/ girlfriend, i.e. flirting
2. Young people sharing the images with someone they are in a relationship with and whom they trust.
3. Young people being tricked into sending the picture to an online predator (not that they know this at the time)

As an adult, we know that none of the above options are really safe, but the consequences for young people when it all goes wrong are disastrous. Young people are trusting, and they want to please others and be liked, but once photos are sent, there is no way to get them back. Once in cyberspace, they become a permanent part of a person's digital footprint. This means they can forever be linked to that person and can resurface when least expected or wanted.

While the immediate fallout is usually among the person's peer group, school and local community, where the pics can then be used to cyberbully and harass the victim, these images can often fall into the hands or onto the computers of those with the predilection to sexually offend against children and young people.

Here is a common scenario I hear all the time:

A young girl is dared by a boy at her school to send a naked pic of herself via Snapchat, but told to only photograph herself from the neck down (hiding the face somehow makes it okay in the minds of some kids). The girl sends the pic and the person receiving it saves it (yes, you can do this on Snapchat, despite what the hype says) then, unknown to the girl, he shares it around in a game called 'Guess who?' It is initially shared with all the boys in his year level; no-one can name the naked person in the picture until one of the female students sees it and quickly identifies the girl with the following comment: 'Oh, that's so and so. Look, there's her athletics trophy in the background.'

How can you avoid this situation?

Know your child's device

Before purchasing a device for your child, or allowing them to use a shared family device, make sure you know how the device works. Look at what the device offers by way of parental controls and restriction passcodes and get the one that has the best security settings. If you are unsure, ask what the device allows to be restricted before purchasing. Many places have free tutorial sessions for purchasers, so sign up and learn before you hand them over.

Regardless of the age of your child, set realistic and clearly defined rules about the use of the device and consider turning things like the camera off via the parental/restrictions settings, but remember that your child probably has a friend with unrestricted access so it must be addressed.

Talk to your child

The best way to minimise your child's risk is to be involved right from the start and keep communicating with them as they get older and become teenagers. A parent has to have many awkward and embarrassing conversations with their children, and of course this one about sexting fits into that category. Parents cannot even rehash the conversation their parents had with them, as this was not an issue twenty years ago. But it's a conversation you must have.

How do you start these conversations? You know your own child or the child in your care, so be guided by their level of understanding, but if they have access to a device that connects to the internet and/or has a camera facility, the time is now.

With younger primary school children I don't use the term 'sexting', but by grades 5 and 6 (eleven to thirteen years) I do talk about a 'naked selfie'. Start by getting out some of their cute baby photos – the ones you plan to use on the slide show at their twenty-first birthday; the embarrassing naked baby in the bath, naked baby at the beach – and talk about why you don't take photos like that now they are at school. Ask them if they would go to sport or another activity without clothes on and why. They will all answer correctly with comments such as its rude, it's not right, it's weird. Praise them for getting the answer correct and discuss how we dress in different ways depending on the situation, such as wearing bathers at the beach. Also mention that Mum and Dad would not go out of the house without clothes on either.

Scenarios

Talking through scenarios works well. An example would be, 'What would you do if someone online asked for a photo of you?' or, 'What would you do if someone asked you to take some clothes off for the photo? Who would you tell?' Of course, the first thing they will reply with is, 'Say no,' as they know it is rude and wrong. The problem is, sometimes when kids are alone and being pressured they don't make the same decisions as they would normally. Also discuss scenarios such as, 'What would you do if someone sent you a pic and you hadn't even asked for it?' and 'What would you do if you knew pics of one of your friends were being circulated?'

What you need is for your child to be comfortable coming to you with anything that is upsetting, especially something online, as it can get out of control quickly. Reassure them that you won't be angry if they tell you about something that happens online. The fear of getting into trouble is an inhibiting factor in kids coming forward with problems. You can make an age-appropriate list of rules and pointers on what to do if something happens online that is not nice. Keep it simple because less is better for young children, so it might just be:

- Say no.
- Put the device down or walk away.
- Tell Mum or Dad (or relevant adult).

Other conversation starters

Talking to teens about anything vaguely embarrassing or awkward is difficult at best but it must be done. Do not put it off because you are embarrassed. Pick your moment. Around the dinner table with little brothers or sisters present or when grandparents are visiting are two examples of when not to discuss this. Find a quiet time with no interruptions or other stresses (such as at exam time or just after a fight with their best friend at school) and talk calmly and rationally.

Most kids don't read newspapers or watch the news, but one way to launch into this topic is to discuss an article in the paper or online. Start with something like, 'Did you see this?' and read part of the article out. Do not be judgemental, or make negative comments such as, 'She must be a slut', or, 'What type of person does this?' because research tells us many kids in many schools are engaging in this behaviour. You don't want to make it worse for your child if they have already had to deal with this or taken a pic themselves. Ask how they feel about it, and if they have heard about it happening at their school, and then lead to a question such as, 'So what would you do if someone asked for a naked pic of you?' Be prepared for them to spit back, 'Say no, of course!', which is the answer you want to hear. It is also how your child believes they would respond. Reality tells a very different story.

Discuss consequences

Conversations about naked selfies need to include possible consequences. Much of the media reporting of these issues brands girls as having their reputations ruined, while boys are nearly always portrayed as the offender with the possibility of facing charges. This skewed reporting does little to help anyone and if you have worked in this space long enough, you will know that labels such as that are plainly incorrect. Both boys and girls can be victims, can be offended against and can be offenders, and either can have reputations ruined. Sadly, however, the perception of a boy sending a dick pic is very different from that of a girl sending a tit pic back to him. It's a double standard, but it's a reality.

Make sure your child knows that they will not get into trouble if they tell you what has happened. This is what kids fear most. Keep the conversation primarily positive and give them the message that no matter what, they can come to you and you will support them. You may need to have several attempts at this conversation, but do not give up.

Take your child's comments and suggestions on board and expand them, praise the positive ones and gently suggest alternatives to any that you can see could lead to problems. These rules can then form part of an online family safety contract (see Appendix 1 for an example). This would include time limits for online use, sites and apps that are permitted, no sharing of personal information online (you may need to discuss what this is), and no talking to or playing games with people you don't know.

A young Year 8 girl that I had helped with a sexting issue wrote the following letter for me to share with parents:

> Last year I moved to high school, and from only having eighteen people in my year to nearly one hundred, it was a change I wasn't prepared for. Many things were yet to come socially that I had no idea about.
>
> Later on that year I started texting a guy I met over the summer holidays. He seemed really nice. The guy ended up asking me for a photo. I didn't know what he was talking about, my face or what … I was incredibly confused. So I asked him, what of? He replied by saying something like 'Take your clothes off,' but I can't really remember. I didn't end up sending him one that night but he didn't let me forget that I said no, he kept on asking me and eventually I did send him one. I think I wanted to feel special.
>
> I didn't realise till later he was not just asking me, he was asking many other girls and I was just another victim.
>
> Weeks later many of his friends started texting me. Obviously finding out what I had done, they wanted a photo too. I liked this one guy that started to text me, I thought he was really cute. He asked me for a photo many times too and promised to send one back, not that I wanted one! He eventually got the better of me and I sent him one too.

He didn't end up sending me one, as his camera didn't work…

I learnt the hard way how to not get caught up in sexting. I regret this so much now and it was just that split second that caught me out to press the send button.

No-one should be treated like I was, I guess it was just the thing all the boys were doing at the time and me and a few of my friends got caught up in it. I think it would have helped me to be aware of what all the sexting stuff was before I entered high school or was around boys with testosterone!

I later found out that my mum had been reading books on teenage girls and even been to my doctor to see why I was acting so rudely. At the time it seemed as though she was always right near me wanting to know everything about what was happening. Yet when I look back she was doing it to help me. One of the girls who was in the boys' grade who I was very close to convinced me to pull away from these boys before they hurt me even more and thanks to her I didn't get even more involved.

I think the best way parents can deal with problems like this is to talk to someone your daughter trusts and who is older than them, like someone in the year above them at school. I found that I trusted her because she was older and knew the boys, and I was close to her because she was in my house at school and also swam. This made it sound cool and reasonable!

Also remember to always remind your child that she is gorgeous and stick up for her no matter what happens!

I think this letter really puts it into perspective. As much as our children tell us that we know nothing about anything, deep down they do rely on us to advise and guide them. Be persistent, consistent and clear.

Naked selfies and the law

One important part of the conversation you have with your child is to explain to them that it is a criminal offence to take, possess or transmit (share via technology) a naked image of a young person (under the age of eighteen years). It doesn't matter how you came to possess the image, or if you willingly took the photo yourself and sent it on. It is still an offence. Let your kids know that:

- **they cannot give themselves** permission to break the law (take pictures of themselves naked or in a sexually explicit way)
- **they cannot give another person** permission to break the law (tell another person that they are fine with it)
- **another person cannot give them** permission to break the law (someone telling them that it is okay). Exceptions are of course if a young person has been tricked, threatened or coerced into sending these images, when they are treated as the victim.

State laws in Australia define a child as being under the age of eighteen years, except for South Australia, where the definition is sixteen years. Commonwealth law that we all must obey defines a child for this purpose as under eighteen years. Under both state and Commonwealth law in Australia, these images are viewed as child pornography. There is no place for discretion, loopholes or other mechanisms to allow perpetrators to have their charges dropped or minimise their role when we are dealing with this sort of crime, but on the other hand, we should not be treating an impulsive young person the same way as a paedophile. Our laws have not kept pace with technology and how that technology is being used. Kids are being charged with the same offences as paedophiles and this is wrong, but at the moment there is no alternative. The state of Victoria has completed a review of these laws, to try to separate sexting behaviour from child pornography images, and eleven out of the fourteen original recommendations have been accepted by the government but are not in statue at the time of writing.

See Chapter 10 for more on the law and cyberspace.

What do I do when a sext has been sent?

- Don't yell, scream or panic. Try to remain calm. It is really important to be able to speak rationally to your child at this time (you can be angry and upset later).
- Talk to them about your concerns or suspicions and allow them time to respond.
- Try to work out how and when this has happened, and who else may be involved. Where are the images now and who may have them? What were the circumstances? Who were they sent to? Have they been forwarded? Are they pics or video (webcam/Skype)? Gather as much information as possible as quickly as possible.
- Make an appointment to speak to someone at the school (the counsellor, their home-room teacher, their year level coordinator or the principal) and let them know what has occurred. This is important so that the school can support your child as required. If they don't know, they can't always guess what is wrong. Also, if the pics are being circulated within the school, they will need to be involved.

- Be aware that in some instances, police may need to be involved and schools do have certain legal obligations in relation to the reporting of incidents. Please don't keep it from the school because you are concerned about police involvement. Police are the best placed to deal with these things and have tools to minimise the impact. Police also have the ability to retrieve data and trace electronic communication. The important thing is to act as soon as you are aware, or if you feel that it is beyond your ability to manage, or if lots of people have the pics.
- Consider other services such a GP for referral to an adolescent psychologist. Some kids get over these things quickly; others don't. Trust your instincts and if your child's demeanour is changing for the worse, act.
- If you believe that the sexting is a result of your child being groomed online rather than adolescent naivety, please refer to Chapter 5 for further advice.

It is imperative that all parents embrace technology for the valuable tool that it is and engage with their children in cyberspace as well as in the real world. Parents should know where their children go and what they do online, the same as in their day-to-day life. Communication is the key, and rules and boundaries about acceptable online behaviours must be put in place. Never threaten total disconnection or removal of technology as punishment for a problem that might arise online. International and Australian research clearly shows that the majority of young people will not tell a parent if they have problems online for fear of losing access. You must encourage your child to tell you about any problems they are having online, or mistakes they have made, without fear of further punishment in the form of removal of access.

The internet and cyberspace are public places. Once images have been posted, they are there forever and no-one can get them back.

Sexting quick-response checklist

- Remain calm.
- Talk to your child about your concerns and give them time to respond.
- Gather as much information as you can as quickly as you can.
- Make an appointment to speak to someone at the school.
- Be aware that the police may need to be involved.
- Consider visiting your child's GP and asking for a referral to a child psychologist.
- If you're concerned that the sexting is due to online grooming, see Chapter 5.

CHAPTER 8

WHY WON'T THEY LOG OFF?

The excessive use of gaming and other internet applications is causing considerable concern among many families worldwide. From first featuring in academic literature by doctors Goldberg, Young and Block in the USA in 1996/97 as an emerging problem, problematic internet use has continued to increase over time. While there have been some recent studies done in relation to the actual problem of internet 'addiction', our understanding mainly comes from anecdotal sources. Much of the focus on internet addiction and children revolves around the playing of games. There are, however, other internet-defined issues that can be described as addictions as well.

Just as not everyone who drinks a glass of alcohol will become an alcoholic, and not everyone who puts $5 into a poker machine will become a gambling addict, we must understand that not everyone who plays an online game will become a gaming addict. There are, however, some key facts that parents must be aware of when deciding if the playing of an online game is a nuisance (to the parent most often), or something much more serious.

There is anecdotal evidence from health practitioners worldwide to demonstrate that serious problems may be encountered when the internet and its apps are misused. Dr David Greenfield from the

Centre for Internet Behavior USA states:

> *The Internet appears to be capable of altering the mood,*
> *motivation, concentration, and producing a dissociating*
> *and disinhibiting experience for users; for some*
> *individuals, patterns of use can transform to abuse, taking*
> *on a compulsive quality ... Many of the daily spheres of*
> *behaviour, including work, appear to be effected by this*
> *powerful technology.*

Too much Minecraft?

A father recently asked me if the fact that his eight-year-old
son played *Minecraft* for four hours per night was a problem.
He went on to say that while he had tried to limit the time
spent playing, his wife had purchased multiple portable
devices, meaning the son could play more easily and he
was becoming very angry when asked to log off. I said that
four hours per night was certainly an issue and needed to
be addressed immediately. We talked about the types of
children most at risk (see more on this on page 104) and
he said that his son was compulsive and a perfectionist,
and wouldn't stop anything until he had it right – all traits
that can be considered risk factors when it comes to the
potential for gaming issues. He then went on to inform me
that his son would get so engrossed in the game that he
would sit and pull his eyelashes out. Now, that is a problem!

In order for a medical practitioner to diagnose a psychiatric or psychological illness, it must be listed in *Diagnostic and Statistical Manual of Mental Disorders (DSM-5)*. In the fifth edition of the DSM, released at the American Psychiatric Association's Annual Meeting in May 2013, Internet Gaming Disorder is identified in Section III as: '. . . a condition warranting more clinical research and experience before it might be considered for inclusion in the main book as a formal disorder'.

Because the disorder is not yet recognised, it cannot be diagnosed, which can pose a problem for patients trying to access medical treatment rebates. It is, however, a well-documented problem around the world, often with tragic consequences. In Asia, for example, there have been many deaths attributed to the continual and excessive playing of online games.

Problem vs addiction

An online game becomes a problem when it has a negative impact on a person's life or that of their family. Often the person playing the game is so engrossed that they do not see the issue. At its worst, playing an online game can take over a person's life to the exclusion of all else. Anecdotally, it is boys who are most vulnerable to developing online gaming issues. Girls tend to not want to log off social networking sites; they want to be connected 24/7. Young males, though, have a clearly defined problem with logging off gaming sites, some becoming agitated and violent and showing signs of clinical withdrawal symptoms when finally disconnected.

There is much dialogue and research about which games are the most addictive and there is no easy answer. Any game can become a problem when it has a negative impact on a person. Online games are cleverly designed to target receptors in the brain; they often work on intermittent reward so that you feel the need to keep playing as you are not sure when you are going to get a bonus. Many also punish you if you log off before *they* want you to. An example is when they revert your score to where you started from if you haven't reached a so-called 'save point'. No-one wants to play for an hour only to find that all the gains made amount to nothing. They also often connect you with other gamers, which means you feel like you need to be online when they are. The problem is that these people are often on the other side of the world so you need to be online when you should be asleep.

Two games that feature consistently in reports of concerning behaviour in young males are *Minecraft* and *World of Warcraft*. This does not mean that the games are bad – not at all – but when time and time again the same games are mentioned it's time to have a look and act if required. In the case of *Minecraft*, it is a very clever, stimulating game with merit, but it does seem to become all-consuming in some kids. *World of Warcraft*, or *WoW* for short, features heavily in medical literature as a game that appears highly addictive and can causes severe psychological problems. In his report for the Swedish Youth Care Foundation, Sven Rollenhagen stated, 'There is not a single case of game addiction that we have worked with in which *World of Warcraft* has not played a part. It is the crack cocaine of the computer gaming world. Some people are literally unable to drag themselves away and will play it till they drop.'

Dr Richard Graham, a psychiatrist and internet addiction expert at the relationship counselling Tavistock Centre in London, said, 'Some of my clients will discuss playing games for 14, 16 hours a day at times, without breaks and without attending to their physical needs . . . For those, the consequences are potentially severe.'

In July 2012, a Taiwanese teenager collapsed and died after playing the game *Diablo 3* for forty consecutive hours. In February the same year another young man died after a 23-hour gaming marathon. Again, not everyone who plays these games is going to have a problem. I am sure some adults find it difficult not to play *Candy Crush Saga* each time they pick up their phone. But you need to know that it's a possibility.

Good gaming practice

Gaming is not all bad! My youngest child learned about maths with *Winnie the Pooh*, and about geography, how to follow a clue and the process of elimination in *Where in the World is Carmen Santiago*, but games have changed. They are no longer a simple disk in a machine, a game with an end. Being able to connect with others around the world while playing the game is both a positive and negative. First of all, when your child wants to play a specific game, you need to have a good look at it yourself. For example:

- What is the game's rating? Remember, M and MA 15+ games are not remotely suitable for primary school-aged children.
- Is it violent? What level of violence is my child exposed to?
- Who does my child connect with?
- Do I think it is suitable for my child and their level of development?
- Are there any known problems with this game? Do your due diligence and search for articles online and via www.commonsensemedia.org.
- Once you are happy for your child to play the game, have a go yourself just to make sure that all is okay.

- Set *very* clear time limits and do not waiver.
- The fact that your child's friends play the game is *not* a good guide as to its suitability for your own child, and regardless of how long other kids game for at night, you need to ensure that the time allocated for your child is reasonable, taking into account age, homework, sport, family activities, bedtime and so on.
- Keep social and homework time separate.
- For younger children, ensure that you know who they are playing with and help them to set their accounts up securely. Make sure there are rules about who they talk to and that they never have private chats outside the gaming environment (grooming takes place in the online game world too).
- Think about the risk factors (see later in this chapter): do any apply to your child?
- Realistic, gory video games, such as the first-person shooter games (for example, *Call of Duty*, *Halo*), should be discouraged because they can lead to desensitisation to violence and aggressive behaviour.
- Games that promote learning academic skills or social cooperation should be encouraged.
- Have a sheet of rules next to the device to ensure your child remembers what is expected.
- Make sure they know they must log off and come and get you if there is anything of concern.
- The minute you feel that the game is taking over, it is time to say no. Online gaming problems often seem to develop almost overnight; it goes from manageable to not manageable very quickly. Be on the ball and don't doubt yourself.

Problem:

At a recent parent seminar I had a mother tell me that she doesn't allow her son to play violent games but rewards good behaviour, completed homework and so on with game time on *Minecraft*. This sounds okay in theory; however, the problem is that now tasks get rushed, showers are so quick that her son doesn't really get wet, and homework is completed in record time, just to get extra time online. While the concept of, 'You cannot game until the task is done,' is admirable, it is now a problem as the game has become the focus, rather than the secondary reward. It's time to enforce a strict gaming time. Tasks must still be completed, but regardless of when the task or homework is done, gaming is at a specified time only, and not every night.

Possible solution:

Sit down and talk about your concerns (your child may not really understand). Explain why you are unhappy and that they seem to be taking advantage of the reward rather than focusing on the tasks. If your child is old enough, ask for suggestions to get gaming time back on track, then work out a suitable compromise. If they are unable to accept their responsibilities, set out clear time guidelines such as:

- home from school, drink, snack, rest
- homework 5–6 pm
- dinner 6–7 pm (technology-free)
- shower etc. 7–7.15 pm
- Minecraft 7.15–7.45 pm
- wind down, quiet time, reading, etc. 7.45–8.30 pm
- sleep.

You need to be flexible to take into account other activities, but at least set a defined start and finish time for games.

Who is at risk?

- **Children who suffer from anxiety:** Children may use games to distract themselves from worries and fears, as an escape from the real world and all its problems. There is also research to show that problematic internet use can lead to anxiety as well.

- **Children who suffer from depression:** The internet can be an escape from feelings of depression, but too much time online can make things worse. Internet addiction further contributes to stress, isolation and loneliness.

- **Children diagnosed with an ADHD-type illness:** Children diagnosed with an ADHD-type illness are known to play online games for longer than those without it, and boys with ASD and ADHD are at greater risk for problematic video game use than are boys with typical development. (*Pediatrics*, Micah O. Mazurek, PhD and Christopher R. Engelhardt, PhD. July 2013)

- **Children diagnosed with Asperger syndrome or an autism spectrum disorder:** These children are known to be compulsive and have limited understanding of social cues, making them more at risk when playing role-playing games.

- **Children who lack social support:** Internet addicts often use social networking sites, instant messaging or online gaming as a safe way of establishing new relationships and more confidently relating to others.

- **'Unhappy' teenagers:** Children might be wondering where they fit in, struggling with identity issues or just having problems at home. When they are online, they feel more comfortable than when they are with their real-life friends.

- **Children who are bored:** If a child feels they have nothing to do, and no interest in anything in the real world, it is easy to lose themselves in the fantasy world of an online game. If it is the only place they are entertained, they are more likely to want to be there.

- **Children who are less mobile (have a physical disability):** These children may not be able to play physical games with their peers or join in due to a disability. Online, they are no different from anyone else, and can excel at a game, which they may not be able to do in the real world. They are not judged by their disability when they are online.

- **Children who are lonely or have few friends in the 'real' world:** Socially awkward or socially isolated young people and teens often find acceptance in the online world that they don't feel in the real world, and may gradually replace the real world with their online world.

- **Children who are stressed:** Some young people use games as an escape from problems. While some use the internet to relieve stress, it can have a counterproductive effect. The longer you spend online, the higher your stress levels will be.

- **Children who show anomie (alienation due to a lack of social norms):** Anomie describes the breakdown of social bonds between an individual and their community. These children are not able to fit in.

What does problematic gaming look like?

- **Losing track of time online:** Does your child frequently find themselves on the internet playing a game for longer than they intended or longer than the allocated time? Does a few minutes turn into a few hours? Do they get irritated or cranky if their online time is interrupted? Do they get angry and abusive if you insist they log off?

- **Having trouble completing tasks on time (homework/ chores):** Do you find your child 'forgetting' or refusing to do their chores because they are playing an online game? Is their homework always being done at the last minute or not at all because they don't seem to have any time to do it? Do they never come for dinner when called?

- **Isolation from family and friends (replacing real friends with only online friends or other gamers):** Is your child's social life suffering because of all the time they spend online? Are they neglecting family and friends? Does your child feel like no-one in their 'real' life understands them like their online friends?

- **Feeling guilty or defensive about the time they spend online:** 'I don't have a problem, you are the one with the problem' is a common response from those displaying worrying online behaviours. Are you sick of nagging your child to get off the computer and spend time as a family or do simple things like eat dinner together? Does your child hide their internet use or lie to you about the amount of time they spend on the computer and what they do while online? Do they log on when they should be asleep or after you have told them no?

- **Only feeling happy when in the gaming environment:**
  Does your child use the internet as an outlet when stressed,
  sad or excited? Have you tried to limit your child's internet
  time but failed? Has your child tried to limit their own time
  but not been successful? Is the only time your child seems
  happy is when they are online?
- **Withdrawal from daily activities:** Does your child seem
  lethargic, not wanting to play sport or do things that
  they used to enjoy? Do they seem uninterested in school,
  and are their grades dropping?

Physical symptoms of spending too much time gaming can include
the following:

- carpal tunnel syndrome (pain and numbness
  in the hands and wrists)
- dry eyes or strained vision
- back aches and neck aches
- severe headaches
- sleep disturbances
- pronounced weight gain or weight loss.

To assist parents and those who care for children, Dr Philip Tam, an
adolescent psychiatrist and an expert in problematic internet use, has
developed the 'i.m.p.r.o.v.e' self-assessment tool, which can be used to
assess internet usage in order to find out if internet use is a problem
and what treatment options should be considered. The diagnostic tool
can be downloaded from the website www.niira.org.au and used by
the young person themselves (for older teens) or by a parent/carer. The
four levels of pathological internet use (PIU) are:

- Level 1 – Mild impact/early problems
- Level 2 – Increased impact/social circle notices (school, peers)
- Level 3 – Clinical impact, specific interventions indicated
- Level 4 – Addiction or PIU, major or whole social role impacted.

The corresponding treatment options for each level of PIU are:

- Level 1 – Self-help, parental assistance, managing it at home
- Level 2 – Associates, school counsellor
- Level 3 – GP, clinical psychologist
- Level 4 – Psychiatric/inpatient plus medication considerations.

Remember, kids often rebel against parents, but a different person saying the same thing can work wonders. If you're worried, trust your instincts and speak to someone.

And finally, we must not overlook the many positive outcomes children derive from playing online games, which in many cases can conveniently be overlooked. It's not all doom and gloom. Through games kids can develop the ability to solve a problem, improve and develop motor skills, learn to care for others, learn responsible behaviour and how to work as part of a team while playing an online game. On the other hand, the negatives are real, and parents need to be aware of all the possible outcomes that come with their child playing online games. The fact is that the same online game can be both amazingly positive and devastatingly negative at the same time.

Internet addiction quick-response checklist

- **Encourage other interests away from the computer:** Make sure your child has a range of different activities that they can participate in, including sporting, cultural and social activities. Find a hobby that they enjoy, join a club, and expose them to a wide range of options. If the first one doesn't work, try again. One is sure to suit.

- **Monitor the device:** Computers, tablets and gaming consoles must be in the common area of the house, so you can monitor both content and usage time. Set clear rules for use including time limits. Consider turning the wi-fi off at say 9 p.m. each night. Set a good example. If you can't or won't log off, your child probably won't either.

- **Use apps and parental controls:** Make sure you take full advantage of the many apps, parental controls and restrictions (see page 133) that are available to limit both the length of time the device is used and the content accessed on smart phones, tablets and computers. You can limit data use, set a specific time of day when access is allowed, such as 7 p.m.–8 p.m., or limit time access, such as thirty minutes. If your child won't log off at the required time, get an app or third-party product that will turn it off for you! (I like a free product called K9 Web Protection, but most reputable filtering companies such as Net Nanny, Kaspersky, Norton, McAfee and so on all have products designed to do this, or simply look online for something that will do what you want.)

- **Talk to your child:** A change in your child's computer use could be the sign of an underlying problem. Are they having problems at school? Are they particularly upset about a family issue? Are they having trouble fitting in and making friends? Are they being bullied online? Are they being forced to play for someone else online? This may be the reason they have retreated into the world of an online game. If you notice any subtle changes in your child's demeanour, then investigate.

- **Ask for help:** While it's pretty straightforward to seek medical advice when our children are sick or injured, it is often hard for parents to seek help when a child has a psychological or behavioural issue. Don't be afraid to ask for help. There are many people who have the expertise to assist parents with any problem their child might be experiencing, including:

  your child's school – they will have access to a range of professionals they can refer you to. The classroom teacher must also be informed so that they can support both you and your child

  your GP, for both advice and referral to a mental health practitioner such as an adolescent psychologist, or visit psychology.org.au

  your local community health centre

  online youth mental health services such as eheadspace.org.au, reachout.com.au or youthbeyondblue.com.

CHAPTER 9

WHAT ELSE IS OUT THERE?

It can be very disconcerting for a parent wandering the murky thoroughfares of cyberspace, wondering exactly what their children are viewing. Are they actively looking for nasty sites? Has a friend given them a website to look up or a word to google? Are they just being naturally curious? Have they innocently accessed unsuitable content? What do I need to worry about?

Of course, the psychological damage access to inappropriate content does will depend on a range of things such as the age of your child, their level of maturity and their state of mental health. Several children of the same age could be exposed to the same content only to have very different responses. You know your child best, so make sure you minimise their access to sites that are clearly not suitable. Making sure they know that your family rules apply wherever they are and whoever they are with is very important, as is letting them know that regardless of what they have seen, or the site they have visited, if they know it was wrong, or the content has upset them, then they must let you know. You in turn must ensure that you do not yell, shout or overreact to a simple mistake or case of curiosity. You are allowed to be angry, upset or disappointed, but you must convey this rationally. If a child thinks a parents' reaction is going to be explosive or scary, they will be less likely to tell you and this can cause further problems because if you don't know, you can't help.

Peer pressure can be highly problematic for children. They have to weigh up 'being part of the cool group' with Mum and/or Dad's rules and expectations. Some children can manage this well; others find it extremely difficult. Sadly, if many of your child's friends are doing the wrong thing online, it can be hard on your child if you say no, and actively parent in cyberspace.

Here is an example of just how many children have no rules for online use placed on them at home. These statistics are from two large suburban primary schools, one in Melbourne and one in Sydney, and are some of the worst I have seen:

- Over 70 per cent of Grade 3 and 4 students were using one or more age-restricted social networking sites.
- 123 out of 140 Grade 5 students were using one or more age-restricted social networking sites.
- 132 out of 160 Grade 6 students were using one or more age-restricted social networking sites.
- 94% of Grade 6 children has one or more age-restriced accounts. Appalling!

Statistics like these make it very difficult for those parents who set rules in place and do not allow their child access to age-restricted sites. These children will clearly be in the minority. No child should ever be made to feel bad for making a good decision, nor should a child be rewarded with a position of leadership in a primary school when they are lying online; this is something that I am trying to get through to school staff. Those awarded the position of school captain should not have fake or underage accounts as it sends a very poor message to the other students: 'it's okay to do the wrong thing online because you can

> The mother of a Grade 6 boy contacted me for advice after her son had been shown extreme violent pornography on an iPod that another student had brought along for the bus ride to school camp. The students had been permitted to bring the devices to listen to music but one boy brought the porn. Her son had been embarrassed and upset by what he saw: women being tied up, gagged and penetrated in multiple places by multiple items, by multiple men. It was scary and as a result he had begun wetting the bed. He could not 'unsee' it and spent the whole camp and several months after severely traumatised.

still get rewarded'. Schools have no hesitation in insisting rules in the real world are obeyed, but they also have a responsibility to ensure that children understand rules regardless of where they are, including the importance of obeying rules online.

I could never list every possible combination of bad things that your child might see or be shown online, nor can I list every website or app that you need to be aware of. However, in this chapter, I will alert you to some of the things that I think parents must currently have a good understanding of:

- pornography
- pro-ana / pro-mia sites
- sextortion
- identity theft
- current apps/sites causing problems.

Pornography

First, you must understand that your child *will* see pornography online. To think otherwise is unrealistic. Whether they go looking for it (most will) or they stumble across it when searching for something else, we know that pornography is both overtly and covertly found online. It can pop up in an innocuous search, for example. A search for something like 'naughty girl' will quickly lead to sexy images and porn websites. Others may look up the word 'pussy' to get a picture of a cute cat for a school project but you can imagine what images will be found with that search. Google the term 'pornography' and you will find around 51300000 results in 0.36 seconds!

Research has found that the age of exposure to pornography is as follows:

- 11 years of age – first exposure to pornography
- 15 years of age – 100 per cent of teen boys have viewed pornography
- 15 years of age – 80 per cent of teen girls have viewed pornography.

The problem is not that pornography is necessarily bad, but that the type of content that impressionable young people are viewing is far removed from anything that would be remotely considered normal. In the past, if a hormonal teenager wanted to view a sexy image their options were limited. They could not purchase it themselves so they had to perhaps sneak a look at Dad's secret stash, grab a sister's *Cosmo* or just simply imagine. If all young boys were looking at was something akin to *Playboy*, then that would not be so bad, but they are not. Research paints a very concerning picture.

A 2009 study by Brown and L'Engle found 'that early exposure to

simple tips to filter adult content and other inappropriate sites

- Set up an account with an internet filtering company such as Open DNS. This will allow filtered content to *all* devices in a home.
- Use a computer filter such as K9 Web protection (this works only on computers, not tablets or smart phones).
- Ask your ISP if they have a modem with parental controls. Some are beginning to provide this service so ask around.
- Set Google SafeSearch. This will cover all Google searches on a device (but only on computers). You must set it up separately for each browser, such as Internet Explorer, Safari, Firefox and so on. Go to google.com.au/safetycenter/.
- Set up Safety Mode on YouTube to ensure inappropriate videos are not accessed. Google SafeSearch and YouTube Safety Mode work together. Turning one on turns the other one and vice versa.
- Put restrictions on child's smart phone so that adult content or specific websites are blocked. The current Apple iOS allows you to list individual websites or click a general adult content block. Android devices have some restrictions available but you can use a third-party product (to purchase, download and add on).

sexually explicit material increases the likelihood that both male and female adolescents will engage in oral sex and sexual intercourse earlier than their non exposed peers'.

Braun-Courville and Rogers (2009) found 'Those who use sexually explicit material are more likely to engage in risky sexual behaviours, such as anal sex, sex with multiple partners, and using drugs or alcohol during sex.'

And collectively, many comprehensive studies have concluded that 'youths that consume pornography may develop unrealistic sexual values and beliefs', and that 'consistent findings have emerged linking adolescent use of pornography that depicts violence with increased degrees of sexually aggressive behaviour'.

Pornography is now portable. It is available any time, anywhere, and kids are bringing it to school on phones, iPods and tablets with increasing frequency. The example below sadly is commonplace.

> A young male sex offender, when asked why he had tied up his girlfriend and forced her to have sex with him, replied, 'In the movies they seem to like it.'

Young boys are being desensitised to violence and the more they watch, the more abusive and graphic the pornography has to be in order to excite them. Continued exposure also gives them a skewed view of normality. Most of the porn that young boys and adolescents watch is abusive and violent, extreme and explicit. Rape, torture and bondage are common themes, often accompanied with close-up images of the female with tears streaming down her face.

This type of pornography shows nothing about love, consent or respectful relationships. Oral sex is not actually considered sex by some teens, more like what kissing was in the 'olden days'. Teenage girls know teenage boys watch porn. They know what a porn star looks like:

perfect figure, hair-free, and of course they never say no. Not that they are actually asked; it is presumed that what will happen will happen. Exposure to pornographic content is manifesting itself in concerning resultant behaviours. A couple of years ago a GP said to me:

> *I am seeing a large number of teenage girls presenting with injuries sustained trying to emulate porn movies. If you or I watched the same video we would know that the body does not do those things without severe pain and that the person in the video was probably drunk, drugged or both. Kids don't have that maturity or life experiences so we are seeing young girls trying the things the boys ask because they don't want to say no.*

There is enormous pressure on girls to perform and conform and unless parents start to step in and provide proper 'sex education' to their children, we will raise a generation of young people who have no concept of acceptable and respectful sexual practices. The earlier a child is exposed to sexual content and begins having sex, the more likely they are to engage in high-risk sex. Research by Dr Jennings Bryant found that: 'More than 66 per cent of boys and 40 per cent of girls reported wanting to try some of the sexual behaviours they had seen online and by high school many of them had.'

Early exposure to sexual content can have a profound impact on children's values, attitudes and behaviours toward sex and relationships. It has never been more important for you to have conversations about sexuality and relationships with your child. Above all else, please don't let the internet be your child's sex educator.

Pro-ana/pro-mia sites

As we all know, there are plenty of not-so-helpful sites online and in fact there are some that are particularly dangerous. Unless you have had cause to deal with these sites, most people have no idea that sites such as those that encourage eating disorders actually exist. A common comment is, 'Why is something so *bad* allowed to be there?'

No one person 'owns' the internet, and although each country has laws about content and tries to classify and identify prohibited content, it is not that straightforward. A lot of objectionable and dangerous content is hosted offshore, which makes it even more difficult for the government here to successfully locate it and request its removal. Ensuring that parents are aware of what is out in cyberspace is vital. You may never need to know about these sites, but then again, one never knows. Forewarned is forearmed.

Pro-ana refers to the promotion of the eating disorder anorexia nervosa. It is often referred to simply as 'ana' and is sometimes personified by anorexics as a girl named 'Ana'. The lesser-used term pro-mia refers to bulimia nervosa and is sometimes used interchangeably with pro-ana. A Google search of pro-ana resulted in about 35000000 results in 0.16 seconds.

These sites are particularly dangerous because as well as peddling medically dangerous advice, most have a live chat facility where users can chat with 'like-minded' individuals or others who will support them in their quest to be thin in the extreme. We know that anorexia nervosa and bulimia are extremely serious and often life-threatening illnesses. Having sufferers accessing these sites can undo all the good work of supportive schools, parents and doctors very quickly. Some of the common things that occur on these sites include:

- endorsing anorexia or bulimia as a highly desirable 'lifestyle' choice
- sharing crash-dieting advice and tips
- providing advice on techniques to avoid food without arousing suspicion
- competing with each other to see who can lose the most weight the quickest
- 'support' for each other by fasting together
- suggesting ways to suppress hunger
- advising each other on how to best induce vomiting
- advising each other on the use of laxatives
- providing advice on how to hide weight loss from parents and doctors
- posting pictures of themselves in order to receive affirmation of their 'beautiful' thin body.

As you can see, the potential damage these sites can cause is enormous. Other similar terms are called thinspiration or thinspo. These sites are often full of pictures of emaciated bodies, which sadly those suffering this illness aspire to be like.

As well as individual websites, these themes are often found within social networking sites. In February 2012, Tumblr announced that it would shut down blogs hosted on its blogging service that 'actively promote or glorify self-harm', including eating disorders, and display warnings on searches for common pro-ana terms. Facebook actively seeks to remove pro-ana content as a breach of its terms and conditions of use in relation to encouraging self-harm in others. However, despite these precautions, there are still plenty of websites where this content can be found.

The message for parents is clear. Be aware of what is out there, especially if your child is becoming increasingly interested in losing weight, has a diagnosed eating disorder or has any mental health concerns. These sites attract vulnerable teens like moths to a light and do enormous harm.

Sextortion

Sextortion is a term invented by the FBI to describe a relatively new type of online crime that began appearing on their radar a couple of years ago. While we have not seen a large number of cases here in Australia yet, there have been several reported cases in the past two years. As many police have no idea about the crime themselves, often cases are misreported or investigated as other crimes.

'Sextortion' is the extortion of an individual that has a sexual component. If demands are not met, the punishment is the posting of pornographic material involving the victim on the victim's (or friends') social networking sites.

Currently, there appear to be two distinct methods used to commit the offence known as sextortion. Following is a description of how each one works:

- Setting up a fake social media account to connect with and gain the trust of a young victim (FBI case study).
- The offender trolls social media and video chat rooms and contacts hundreds of young girls while waiting for one to take the bait.
- The offender uses methodically scripted conversations that turn personal after trust is gained.
- Questions about bra size, sexual history and other personal questions ensue.

- If simple pictures were sent, the offender demands more revealing ones.
- After the victim complies (many do out of fear), the offender threatens to destroy their reputation by publishing the pictures or posting them online, unless more and more are sent. The victims go along with it out of fear and are willing to do everything asked to protect their reputation.

4. Sending a malware (virus) to the victim's computer via an email attachment that gives the offender remote access to the device and everything on it. This method also allows the offender to remotely activate the webcam.

- The offender conducts research on the victim through the use of social networking sites, then contacts the victim via email/instant messenger.
- The email has the malicious software embedded into it and the victim's computer is now controlled ('owned') and monitored by the offender, who has access to all files, photos, videos and the webcam on the victim's computer.
- The offender searches for pornographic photos the victim may have taken in the past and then 'sextorts' them by demanding further pornographic material from the victim, or threatens to post the material on the victim's (and/or friends') social networking sites.
- The malicious software allows the offender to see all the victim's computer activity. If the victim attempts to reach out for help, deletes files or emails friends, the offender contacts them immediately, indicating knowledge of their attempt for help. This further alienates the victim, forcing them to comply with the sextortion demands.

- Once one victim's computer is controlled, the offender will reach out to the victim's friends via social networking sites or email accounts representing themselves as the victim in an effort to further spread the sextortion scheme.

Simple tips to prevent sextortion

Don't take for granted that your computer's anti-virus software is a guarantee against intrusions. Turn off your computer when you aren't using it.

Cover your webcam when not in use. Sticky tape or Blu Tack work well.

Don't open attachments without independently verifying that they were sent from someone you know.

It's okay to be suspicious. If you receive a message with an attachment from your mother at 3 a.m., maybe the message is not really from Mum. Many people are too trusting when it comes to their computers.

If your computer has been compromised and you are receiving extortion threats, speak up and inform police.

Identity theft

Identity theft should be a concern for everyone who uses the internet, including young people. They often live their life online and regardless of age, having one's identity stolen can be emotionally and financially devastating. Well-organised criminal gangs trawl the internet and social networking sites just to see what they can find. Many will gather and collate information on young users and keep it until the person turns eighteen, when it can be more useful to them. They then use

Tips to protect your child's identity online

- **Stop and think before you share any personal or financial information about you, your friends or family.** Don't disclose identity information (driver's licence, Medicare number, birth date, address) through email or online unless you have initiated the contact and you know the other person involved.
- **If you use social networking sites, use the highest possible security settings.** Be truthful when you set the account up, but then hide all identifying information from public/friend view.
- **Don't give your email address out without needing to.** Think about why you are providing it, what the benefit is for you and whether it will mean you are sent emails you don't want.
- **Before giving your email address online, read the website privacy policy.** This should tell you how they will use the email address you provide.
- ***Never* send credit card account information via email.** Only use a credit card to pay for something via a secure online site. Look for the padlock or other sign that the payment portal is secure.
- **You may want to have a second email account.** Use your primary email with friends and businesses you know and trust and have a different one for social networking accounts, subscribing to sites, loyalty programs and so on.
- **Set strong passwords, particularly for important online accounts, and change them regularly.** These should be changed four times per year and should contain a mixture of upper-case and lower-case letters, numbers and symbols.

the stolen information to obtain credit or loans and may run up huge debts in the young person's name. They may also conduct illegal activities in their name. If they have gained enough information to access the young person's accounts, they can steal their money and ruin their credit rating. Parents must ensure that from a very young age, their children understand what personal information is and the importance of *not* sharing it online, even if they know the other person. Being cautious online is a very good habit to get into.

New apps and websites

As I have previously said, it is impossible to give you a definitive list of everything you need to try to avoid. Some sites are quite okay if used correctly, but if used incorrectly may cause harm. On pages 49–51 I discuss the sites that are *most commonly reported to me* as problematic for children. These are the ones that most frequently come to my attention because schools seem to be dealing with them on a daily basis because of misuse.

Please note that many of these sites will probably be replaced by something else in the future, but new sites and apps tend be run the same way and to have the same problems; they just have new names. Just recently, I have become aware of several new apps making news in the USA and UK. One common feature of these apps is the perception of anonymity and also the idea that the messages 'delete' (this is not the case; they just can't be seen on the screen).

Of course, if every site and app was used correctly by all users, then there would be no 'bad' sites. People wouldn't bully or harass, predators would not lurk and content would be clearly marked so that parents could make quick and easy decisions. If only!

Site	Description	Age
Confide	A messaging app that allows users to create and send messages that when viewed, disappear. It allows screen capture of the message and will alert the sender that this has been done. Confide encourages users to 'go off the record' and 'say what you like' as the message is confidential, but as we know nothing is truly confidential online.	13+
Omegle	Omegle is a free online chat website that allows users to communicate with strangers without registering. The service randomly pairs users in one-on-one chat sessions. Its tag line is 'talk to strangers'. Enforce the age restriction for your child.	17+
Popcorn Chat	Allows users to privately chat with people within a 1 mile (1.6 kilometre) radius. Its purpose is to allow you to immediately discover who is around you. Do you want this for your child? Its iTunes app description also encourages students to use the app at school when they are bored!	13+
Secret	Allows people to anonymously post anything. It's not so secret in the end, with comments able to be traced.	13+

Telegram	Similar to sending an SMS to your phone contacts, but it also supports group messaging for up to 200 people. Much like other messaging apps, however, the main concern here is the ability for users to set up 'Secret Chat', which includes a self-destruct timer that removes any message sent using the feature from both devices within a timescale of between two seconds and one week.	13+
Whisper	A free social networking app that encourages users to share secrets anonymously, as well as chat with other 'whisperers'. If your location services are on, then your location shows up on the list of nearby 'whispers'.	13+ but rated as suitable only for those aged 17+
WUT	In order to use the WUT app you need a Facebook page, but which when downloaded allows the user to send out anonymous messages to all your Facebook friends. The messages are silent so your child's phone will not even vibrate.	13+

CHAPTER 10

WHAT YOU CAN DO

What you can do It would be great to be able to provide a template that all parents could follow with the result that their children would be safe online. Sadly, this is not possible, nor is it realistic. Families are different, kids are different, homes are different, and this is why each parent needs to be able to look at what the issues are for their children and act accordingly. Even if you are not sure what you should be doing, or what the real dangers are, then following the steps below will stand you in good stead. Remember, you cannot achieve 100 per cent safety online, but you can get close. Please don't think, 'Not my child', as there are thousands of parents who in hindsight wished they had acted sooner rather than reacted afterwards. Some of the following tips are simple common sense, some are creative and some will require time and patience in order to achieve the desired outcome. Don't falter, stay strong and know that you are doing the right thing.

Simple steps to help keep your child safe in cyberspace

- **Get the tech stuff out of the bedroom:** As much as we think we can, no parent can monitor what is going on behind a closed door or in a bedroom. All internet-enabled devices (iPad, phone, iPod, Xbox) should be in a common area of the house but you still need to check what is going on. There is also the issue of sleep hygiene and excessive screen time. Kids (and adults) need quiet time away from bright screens and the temptation to text a friend before falling asleep. Even if your child has no interest in texting or communicating at 2 a.m., there are plenty of kids who do and will happily bombard friends with messages all night. Take the temptation away. Lead by example and put all devices on charge on a power board in the kitchen overnight. Hand them back after everyone has eaten breakfast.

- **Parental monitoring is vital:** Walk past your child and see what they are doing, who they are talking to and what sites they are on. Be wary if their mood changes, if they become more secretive or if they get jumpy when you walk by. This is *not* invading their privacy – it is parenting in the digital space. Have a rule that when you walk by to check the screen they must put the device down so that you can see. This prevents quick hands minimising or shutting down apps. If they break the rule, have a consequence. Do not, however, spend too long reading everything that they are doing. Check that they are doing what they have told you, are on a site you approve of and chatting to someone you actually know, then praise them and move on.

- **Don't over monitor:** You will need to monitor very young children much more than older children, but remember the older child must have obtained your trust by doing the right thing over a sustained period of time. One good decision is not enough and you still must check. Just because you are their 'friend' on social media or 'follow' them does not mean you will see everything that goes on, but you will see a fair bit. If you see something that you don't like, *do not* make an online comment; speak directly to your child. Do not punish them if a 'friend' does something you don't like. It is not your child's fault. Remember, no-one wants a Facebook-stalking mum or dad, so no comments, and no friend request to their friends. Just sit back, watch and act if required.

- **Don't respond to abuse:** Make sure your child does not respond to rude or harassing comments as this will only make it worse. Ensure that your children know to come and get you immediately if something upsets them online, whether it's something directed at them or a friend. Make sure that you as the parent/carer don't jump on and fire abuse back either, or post nasty and bullying comments about other kids and their parents online from your account. This will not help, and remember that you are the adult and should know better. It's easier said than done, but do try to set a good example.

- **Report the abuse to the site:** All legitimate sites have terms-and-conditions-of-use rules that state the site will not tolerate harassing and bullying behaviour. The problem is that on most sites it is not prevented; it happens, then you report it, then they act. Often this process is slow and further abuse can occur, but this is slowly improving. You must, however, report it to them as soon as possible. On Facebook, you can follow the progress of your report via the Support Dashboard and they will let you know the outcome. If you are not happy you can send it back for review. You can also let a friend know you are upset via the 'Trusted Friend' tool, which in turn generates a Facebook report as well. Make sure that your child knows how all the safety and reporting features of a site work before letting them have an account. Sit together and have a play around with the settings and learn together what to do if there is an issue before it occurs. Prevention is better than cure.

- **Block and delete:** If your child is having problems on social media or gaming sites, make sure that as well as reporting the comment to the site, you block the person being abusive. This option can be called block, delete or ignore. Don't let the bully remain in contact with your child, which means blocking or removing them as friends or contacts for all accounts.

- **If harassment continues:** You may need to close accounts down or change a phone number. It's a nuisance when you have done nothing wrong, but when making a decision about safety, sometimes it just has to be done. Accounts can be set up again if desired, but make sure that you invest the time and energy in making use of all the inbuilt safety and security settings. The new account details should only be given to a selected few. If you have to change your phone number because of abuse, it must be done for free. Consider silent and unlisted numbers and non-identifying pictures on social networking sites.

- **Keep a copy:** The first thing anyone will ask when you are reporting online abuse to them (whether it is the school, a sporting club or the police) is, 'Do you have a copy?' Copy and paste the comment to another document and save it, take a screen shot of it or perhaps print a copy. Use whatever method you are comfortable with. Don't delete it if it is serious enough to take to the school or police. While police can retrieve most if not all content, it does make the initial investigation easier if they can see it in the account, or on the phone. Schools, workplaces and sporting clubs will rely on what you can show them. If you see something abusive about another person and you are not sure they can see it, keep a copy as well, to assist them with their report. Don't be afraid to send copies of abuse directly to the school so that they can be aware of what is going on, even if your child is not involved.

- **Advise your child to immediately exit any site that makes them feel uncomfortable or worried:** Teaching children to understand their early warning signs and to trust their instincts is vitally important. It is also very hard and kids' brains are simply not developed enough to always get this right. Make sure that they know they can come and tell you something that has bothered them without getting into trouble. It may be nothing, but better to have lots of false alarms than a disaster.

- **Have a family internet contract:** Have a set of clear guidelines or house rules about what information your child can put onto websites or share with others. Include the accounts that they are permitted to have, who they can chat to, what apps and games they can play, asking permission before doing something new, and when and how long they can spend online. Also have consequences for breaking the rules. You need to be in charge. (See page 141 for a sample contract.)

- ***Never* threaten total disconnection:** It is very easy as a parent to simply say, 'Okay, that's it. No more phone, internet, iPod, etc. Ever.' It's sort of like when your parents told you that you were grounded *forever*! Who were they kidding? Anyway, when threatened with total disconnection, kids will often not tell you about issues. They would much rather put up with the bad to keep the good. Removal of tech privileges for breach of rules, homework not being done or fighting with a sibling is not a problem, but beware the threat of total disconnection!

- **Tell them you will help them no matter what:** Make sure your children understand that they will not get in trouble if they tell you about a problem, or about something they have seen or done online. Kids really do fear this. Even as a victim, kids will blame themselves or think it is their fault, meaning punishment. It's often an overreaction but hey, we are talking about kids.

- **Monitor your child's phone plans:** Regularly check their phone plans, credit use and calls out where possible. Be alert for any changes, peaks in usage that seem unusual or calls or texts to numbers you don't know.

- **Learn the lingo:** Parents must learn about the internet with their child – get your kids to share their knowledge of the internet with you in a fun environment. Spend time online with your children, just as you would with many other activities such as sport, board games and walking the dog – learn and explore together. Familiarise yourself with the common internet terms and abbreviations (See Chapter 11).

- **Need and want:** The cry commonly heard when a parent wants to get their children off the internet, or threatens to turn the wi-fi off, is, 'But I need it to do my homework.' That is, of course, not true, but it's something many parents seem to believe. There is a very big difference between the words *need* and *want*, and kids do confuse them. Kids will need some 'connected' time to download a sheet, search the net for a project and so on, but to actually do the project, they don't need to be connected. They don't need the internet to write the essay or do the maths sheet, but they will tell you they *need* to be connected because they *want* to be so that they can chat on Facebook while writing the essay! With older teens, be aware that for group assignments they may need to be online and being able to chat with a classmate is often a help. Just make sure they don't abuse the privilege.
- **Install filters:** Make sure that all devices your child uses have monitoring and blocking software installed where possible to minimise dangers. This is already done in schools, but homes should have up-to-date filtering software installed. Remember that you cannot put a traditional filter on a phone or tablet, so look at what parental controls are available via restrictions or other similar settings. Filters *can* sometimes fail to protect and can be bypassed by a child who knows their way around technology.
- **Know the device:** If you are going to give your child an electronic device to use, either a family device or one of their own, then make sure you have a good working knowledge of it. Know what it does and what it is capable of doing. Can it connect to the internet? Can apps be downloaded? Can your child chat with others? Smart phones are mini computers and

kids rarely use them to make phone calls. In fact, if you see a child or teenager talking on a phone it will most likely be to Mum or Dad!

- **Use parental controls:** Most gaming consoles will have some form of parental controls that allow you to set and restrict certain things. Your TV has a parental lock system and many phones and tablets have a separate layer of control available by entering a restriction passcode. Things that you can control on an iPhone, for example, include turning the camera off (so no naked selfies), limiting apps to a certain age rating, prohibiting in-app purchases (you must do this to avoid getting a massive bill), stopping them adding new friends in games and much more. Check them out prior to purchase so you get the one that is best suited to you. You may like to consider an add-on program that can limit access to the internet by length of time or time of day. Others can allow parents to set controls about what numbers can ring a phone, text a phone and so on. Apple stores have regular free tutorials for their products so sign up for one and learn. For other devices, visit the website or ask the person selling the device. If they cannot assist, go elsewhere.

- **Turn off location services:** Having location services active on a smart phone can allow people to find out exactly where your child is at any given time. Smart devices include built-in geolocation technologies that allow you to identify the physical location of the device. Even some digital cameras offer this; when you are taking a pic your exact location comes up on the bottom of the screen. This can provide other people using the same applications as your child with real-time access to your child's location. Having this option turned on also allows for the location information to be contained in the metadata that is hidden inside a digital image. If these images are posted online then a simple scan of the metadata will tell someone where the picture was taken. You have to weigh up the risk of this option as most kids want them turned on so that they can check into locations and tell friends where they are. Some Systems now allow the GPS to be on but off for the camera setting, for example. Unfortunately, they could also be telling the wrong person. Online child sex offenders use this routinely to locate children. Be aware.

- **Set time limits:** Be very clear about how long your child can spend online and what they can do. Try to keep social/game time separate from homework and study time. Set up a mutually agreeable timetable, but school work must come first. It's all about balancing the need for play, rest, homework, sport and so on. When tech time takes over, or begins to have a negative impact on the family, it's time to say no.

- **Know the sites they use:** Ignorance is no excuse. If your child is using it, playing it or chatting on it, you need to know what it is and what it does. Are there privacy settings? Who can access your child? Who can your child access? Is the content suitable? Can certain things be restricted? Is there an age restriction? What is the age rating for the site or app? Google the site or app and check for yourself; don't rely on the positive review your child gives you. Ask your child's teacher if they have seen any problems with a particular site or app. If you don't like it, don't think it is age appropriate or think it is an unsafe place for your child to be, then say no.

- **Check their profiles:** Regularly check all the accounts your child has, especially their social networking ones, to ensure that the content is suitable and that pics and videos posted are not sexy or flirty. Kids don't see things the same way adults do, so they often need guidance about how others would see them and what messages they may unknowingly be giving to others. Also regularly check the security and privacy settings to ensure they are as secure as possible. Non-identifying pictures are often a good thing and using their correct age on sites such as Facebook is important for the stronger default security settings.

- **Keep personal information private:** Make sure that your child knows what personal information is (their name, street address, date of birth, phone number, email address and school) and why it should not be shared online. Make sure they get your permission *before* entering information into online accounts so you can assess whether the site or account is suitable. This is a good reason to set up all your young children's accounts through your email address. I also suggest using a parent's work address when street addresses *must* be included. For older teens, make sure you have the password for their email accounts. Kids often think that the definition of privacy is keeping things from Mum and Dad!

- **Obey the age restrictions on sites:** As mentioned, many sites, especially social networking sites, have legally binding age restrictions. This is usually the age of thirteen years and is derived from the *Children's Online Privacy Protection Act* (COPPA) in the USA but is applicable to Australian users. Apps and games will also have ratings, so check those out before you allow your child to play the game. Allowing children to believe that online rules don't matter is not good parenting and causes confusion in children. Lying online can be very serious, especially if kids grow up believing it is okay. Apart from the legal considerations, most of these sites are simply not suitable for children regardless of whether you monitor them or not (and of course you should); older teens also need to be monitored. If kids in primary school could manage the online interactions these sites allow, then primary school principals would not be spending part of every day dealing with issues arising from the use of age-restricted sites. Popular sites with age restrictions of thirteen years and over are: Facebook, Instagram, Kik (rated as suitable for 17+), Snapchat, iTunes, YouTube (to be an account holder) and many more. Don't support your child to break the rules and know that they won't be the only one without these accounts. Learn to say no.

- **Set social networking profiles to private:** All social networking sites, apps, photo and video sharing and so on must be set to private. Use all the security settings available to make the site as safe as possible. Remember, nothing is 100 per cent safe and even the best settings are not a guarantee that there will not be problems; it is about minimising the risk. Be truthful about your child's age as some offer teen account holders stricter default settings than adult account holders. If you don't want your friends seeing your other friends, set this setting to 'only me'. There are lots of things you can do to protect your privacy. Most take considerable time and effort but the results will be absolutely worth it.
- **Only interact with people you know:** Social networking 'friends' should be people that your child knows in real life and people that they know to *your* satisfaction. This is one

way to reduce possible risks, because as discussed, anyone can be anyone online. Just because someone else appears to know the person, this does not mean it's okay to accept a friend request. An online friend that you don't know in the real world is actually a stranger and should be treated as such. Many online predators gain access to kids because once one person accepts them, they have become a 'friend in common'. It is common practice among kids and teens to blindly accept a friend request that comes from someone who has one or more friends in common. Teach your children that this is dangerous and they should actually know the person first, in the real world, and not take someone else's word for it.

- **If it's too good to be true . . . :** We all know the saying, 'If it seems too good to be true, it probably is'; this applies online as much as anywhere. Make sure your children know about online scams. Teach them that they are not to click on any links or pop-ups without telling you first. Teach them also that they are never going to be the '1 millionth visitor' to a site or win an iPad every day, and that celebrities are not going to send friend requests to them. These things are very tempting to children (and some gullible adults), so keep the conversation going.

- **Use strong passwords:** Passwords are the key to online security so make sure your child uses them. They are like the front door or car key, or your EFTPOS card's pin number. Make sure that the password is strong (many sites rate the strength) and that it is changed regularly. A password should not be something that anyone else knows about your child, like their favourite footy team or pet's name, or something that could be guessed such as their favourite food. Make sure that you know all your child's passwords or passcodes (for a phone or tablet), but make sure that your child knows not to share them with others. Kids see passwords as a commodity to be shared, a measure of a friend, and they do share them, willingly or under duress. Kids worry that if they share a password with Mum or Dad, they will spend all day logging on pretending to be them! That's obviously wrong, but it does come down to trust. An email recently from a young girl who had her account hacked shows just how trusting kids are. She told me up-front that she had given her password to her three best friends, and then all her settings were changed, pornography sites and other sites were followed and the email address linked to the account was changed. When I told her that it would have to be one of her friends, her response was, 'But there are my best friends.' Yes, but best friends sometimes betray you. Don't risk it.

- **Trusting older children:** For older children, who don't want Mum or Dad snooping on them online, I suggest that they write their passwords on a piece of paper and put it in an envelope with their name on it. Seal it and draw thick texta lines several times on the back and over the seal. This will clearly show if someone has tried to open the envelope. Put the envelope in a mutually agreed safe place (make sure you write that down in case it is so safe you forget!). Your child can check regularly that you have not breached their trust, but you can be reassured that if something is not right, you can log on and check.

- **Multi-step log-in:** Many sites offer multi-step log-in. Banks have been doing it for a while; you have to log on to your internet banking account with a username or account reference and password, and then before you can make any transaction to an account outside your own, you enter an SMS code that the bank sends to your mobile phone. Others have a token system for larger transactions where you have to enter the number on a token. Social networking accounts such as Facebook also offer multi-step log-in. A couple of additional seconds spent logging on with an extra step can save hours of anguish later.

- **Log on, log off:** For ease of access most kids (and some adults) leave themselves logged on to sites or they check the box that logs them in automatically. While this is quick and simple, it is not as safe as completely logging off and then on again next time you visit the site. Ensuring your child develops good online habits is vital. This must be one of them, and make sure you lead by example.

- **Turn the webcam off:** Webcams are great for keeping in contact with those who aren't close by, even friends in the next street, and now nearly every device has an inbuilt webcam facility. Just as we log on and off different sites, we should turn on the webcam when required and off when not in use. The increase in cases where viruses have been sent to people's computers that manually allowed access to a webcam is concerning. To safeguard against that, put a small piece of tape or Blu-tack over the camera when not in use.

- **Just because it's online doesn't mean its okay:** Teach children that information on the internet is not always reliable. Things may not be as they seem; people and sites can be untruthful just as some people are dishonest in the real world. Teach them that the first option that comes up on a Google search may not be what they were actually looking for. Teach them about safe surfing and use inbuilt content filters such as YouTube's Safety Mode or Google Safe Search to further protect them.

- **Supervise supervise, supervise:** Very close supervision for young children is recommended and young children should not aimlessly surf the net. Parental supervision is very important but of course you cannot be there 24/7. Have a family online contract, as mentioned earlier, and then develop a system that works for your family. Did the kids go online when you were at work after you told told them not to? Change the wi-fi password every morning and don't give it to them until you are home at night. They won't log off at a certain time at night? Again, change the password or simply turn the internet off at the switch. Your child gets up in the night to turn the internet back on? Take the modem to bed for a cuddle! I was regularly getting little messages from a close friend's young daughter who has worked out how to use iMessage. Mum and Dad are often sound asleep when said daughter, who is awake early, sneaks into their bedroom and 'borrows' the iPad. Wi-fi is now turned off each night. The possibilities are endless. Whatever works for you is fine.

- **Ask for help:** If you are unsure or need assistance in parenting your child online, there are many places to find help. The internet itself is full of useful (and not so useful) information, so check out my list of handy websites (Chapter 11). Schools are another good source of information. Remember that education is a partnership; they want your child to be happy as well, so if you're struggling or not sure, please ask. They often have dedicated IT staff who can also point you in the right direction. Other parents are often a good source of information, as are online forums. Be aware, however, that some do provide dangerous advice, so check the credentials of anyone commenting or offering advice on cyber issues. Just because a blogger has lots of followers does *not* mean they are experts in anything. Many places offer idealistic advice, which in the real environment is not at all helpful.

The internet and its various applications are a lot of fun and a wonderful tool . . . maximise the benefits and surf safely together. But please note that this list is by no means exhaustive and there is no guarantee that following these tips will provide 100 per cent protection or safety for those using the various applications of the internet.

Online family safety agreement (parents)

The internet and digital technology is a wonderful thing and as a family we will need to work together and support each other to make good decisions about what we do online, where we go and what to do if there is a problem. Working together is the best way to make sure that the whole family is as safe as possible when online. This agreement sets out our very clear rules and expectations for both the adults and the children in our family.

I, _____ , as the parent, carer or guardian of _____ , agree that:

- I will teach my child good online habits by modelling acceptable behaviour myself when online.

- I will learn how each device works before giving it to my child to use.
- I will install or activate parental controls, restrictions and/or filters as are applicable for the age of my child.
- I will try my best to keep up with all the websites, apps, games, etc. that my child may want to use and explain rationally why I may say no to a certain site or app. This is my responsibility as a parent.
- I will set up accounts on all the sites, games and apps that my child has so that I can ensure that the communication is suitable and so I can be part of their digital world.
- I will engage with my child online, and play games with them just as I would in the real world.
- I will set clear rules and boundaries about what they can do online, where they can go and for how long. This can be amended for both good and bad online behaviour at any time.
- I will set specific technology-free times, such as before school, during meals or Sunday afternoon, for example. I will also obey this rule.
- I will know all my children's email addresses and passwords in case of emergency. I will not use them unless absolutely required if I believe my child may be in danger or behaving inappropriately online.
- I will not be a Facebook stalking parent. I will not post pictures or comments that could embarrass my child, I will not add my children's friends to my account and I will not comment on things I see but speak privately to my child if required. I will not be angry with my child for what someone else posts to their account.
- I will ensure that all internet-enabled technology is kept out

of the bedroom. Phones will be handed to me at _____ p.m. each night and charged with all other phones. They will be given back at a suitable time the following morning. iPods will not be allowed in bedrooms unless the home wi-fi is switched off first.

- I will ensure that my child is not using apps or websites that have age restrictions that are older than they are.
- I will ensure that my child knows what to do if they have a problem online or see something that they know is wrong. I promise to support them and assist them regardless, and they will know that they can come to me if they have any problems about anything.
- I will assist my child to keep a copy of and report all inappropriate online behaviour to the site in question, the school, the sport club and/or the police. I will teach my child that misusing technology can be a criminal offence.
- I will embrace and enjoy technology just as my child does!

Signed _____

(Parent/Guardian/Carer)

Online family safety agreement (child)

I, _____ ,

aged _____ years, agree that:

- I will obey all the rules of this agreement and understand they have been set with my safety in mind.
- I will not start any new accounts, download any apps or play any online games without first asking permission from my parents.
- I will not start any new accounts or download any apps that have an age restriction older than me.
- I will not talk online to people that I do not know in the real world, even if my friends do.
- I will choose a sensible screen name and email address that does not include reference to my location or my age.
- I will teach my parents as much as I can about the internet and digital technology as it is a lot of fun. I will help them understand things if they are unsure.
- I will not share my passwords with anyone other than my parents. This includes my friends. I understand that my parents will not use them except if they feel I am in danger. I will make sure my parents know what accounts I have, what each user or screen name is, and my email address.
- I understand that there are crimes online and that I can get into a lot of trouble if I misuse technology.
- I will use technology with respect and responsibility.
- I will use my manners and be polite when I am online. I will not swear or use mean words and I will not join in if others are being nasty. If I see cyberbullying I will log off and tell an adult.

- I will immediately log off and tell my parents if I see something online that is scary, mean or not nice, or something that worries me.
- I will obey my parents' rules for no technology in bedrooms and at certain 'no technology' times of the day. I will log off when my online time is up or if asked to.
- I will never agree to meet someone that I have only met online. I know that some people online are not who they say they are. I will tell my parents if someone asks to meet me.
- I will tell my parents if someone asks to do something that I know is not right or something that bothers me. I will not use the webcam with people that I do not know in the real world.
- I will not send pictures of myself with my clothes off or in my underwear. I will immediately tell my parents if I am asked to do this.
- I will tell my parents if I receive rude or naked pictures of anyone.
- I will not post things online that I would not say in the real world.
- I will not share personal information online unless my parents say it is okay. This means I do not share my name, address, mobile and home phone number, school, sport club, teachers' names or screen names.
- I will not open any emails or click links or pop-ups that are from people I have not met in the real world.
- I will try to be a good and responsible digital citizen and as a family we will learn and have fun together online.

Signed _____
(Child)

Cyberspace and the law

Despite what some people believe, cyberspace is not devoid of laws and there are actually many laws to protect users from those who may choose to use technology to bully, harass or otherwise misuse it. There is, however, a distinct lack of knowledge, understanding and application of these laws Australia-wide. This stems mainly from the fact that the words 'cyberbullying' and 'sexting' do not appear in legislation. Cyberbullying is a course of conduct and this then fits within the provisions of state and territory stalking offences. Sexting offences fall within the child pornography laws. Victoria is the only state with a specific state law, known as Brodie's Law, which can be applied to cyberbullying offences. Victoria is also leading the way in relation to amending legislation to provide for a separation of sexting and child pornography laws, so that young people sending a naked picture of themselves are not treated the same way as a paedophile. Victoria is also looking at a new law that would make it illegal to share intimate photos of another person without their permission. This proposed law would apply to children as well as adults.

We must ensure that all technology users, especially young people and their parents, know what the laws are, what constitutes an offence and what the penalties can be.

In Australia, there are two tiers of laws: state and Commonwealth. Most of the day-to-day laws that form the basis of a safe community come from individual state and territory law; however, there are some areas of Commonwealth law that are used regularly to prosecute individuals (technology legislation in particular). If you reside in the Australian Capital Territory, you will rely solely on Commonwealth laws.

Following is a list by state or territory of the most commonly used laws for the offences of:

- cyberbullying
- child pornography
- sexting
- posting threats online.

Please note that this is not an exhaustive list and each case reported to police is evaluated in relation to the most appropriate laws. Although each state and the Northern Territory has a law that can be used for the prosecution of cyberbullying offences, they also rely heavily on Section 474.17 of the *Commonwealth Criminal Code Act* 1995, '*Use a carriage service to menace, harass or cause offence*'. In relation to the sexting laws, all states except Western Australia have state/territory provisions as well as being able to prosecute using commonwealth legislation. It is not uncommon to see an offender charged with both state and commonwealth offences together.

Australian Commonwealth legislation

Legislation that can be used for cyberbullying or online threats:

Using a carriage service to menace, harass or cause offence
Commonwealth Criminal Code Act 1995 (Cth) s 474.17

Using a carriage service to make a threat
Commonwealth Criminal Code Act 1995 (Cth) s 474.15

Legislation that can be used for sexting/child grooming & child pornography offences:

Using a carriage service for child pornography material
Commonwealth Criminal Code Act 1995 (Cth) s 474.19

Possessing, controlling, producing, supplying or

obtaining child pornography material for use through a carriage service
Commonwealth Criminal Code Act 1995 (Cth) s 474.20

Using a carriage service to procure persons under 16 years of age
Commonwealth Criminal Code Act 1995 (Cth) s 474.26

New South Wales legislation

Legislation that can be used for cyberbullying or online threats:

Intimidation
Crimes Act 1900 (NSW) s 545AB

Legislation that can be used for sexting or child pornography offences:

Production, dissemination or possession of Child Abuse Material
Crimes Act 1900 (NSW) s 91H

Northern Territory legislation

Legislation that can be used for cyberbullying or online threats:

Unlawful Stalking
Criminal Code Act 1983 (NT) s 189

Legislation that can be used for sexting or child pornography offences:

Possession of Child Abuse Material
Criminal Code Act 1983 (NT) s 125B

Publishing Indecent Articles
Criminal Code Act 1983 (NT) 125C

Using a child for the production of child abuse material
Criminal Code Act 1983 (NT) s 125E

Queensland legislation

Legislation that can be used for cyberbullying or online threats:

Unlawful stalking

Criminal Code 1899 (Qld) s 395E

Legislation that can be used for sexting/child grooming & child pornography offences:

Involving a child in making child exploitation material

Criminal Code 1899 (Qld) s 228A

Making child exploitation material

Criminal Code 1899 (Qld) s 228B

Distributing child exploitation material

Criminal Code 1899 (Qld) s 228C

Using the internet etc. to procure children under 16

Criminal Code 1899 (Qld) s 218A

South Australian legislation

Legislation that can be used for cyberbullying or online threats:

Unlawful Stalking

Criminal Law Consolidation Act 1935 (SA) s 19AA

Unlawful Threats

Criminal Law Consolidation Act 1935 (SA) s 19

Legislation that can be used for sexting or child pornography offences (child defined as under 16 years):

Production or Dissemination of Child Pornography

Criminal Law Consolidation Act 1935 (SA) s 63

Possession of Child Pornography

Criminal Law Consolidation Act 1935 (SA) s 63A

Tasmanian legislation

Legislation that can be used for cyberbullying or online threats:

Stalking

Criminal Code Act 1924 (Tas) s 192

Legislation that can be used for sexting or child pornography offences:

Producing, distributing, possessing, accessing etc.

Child Exploitation material.

Criminal Code Act 1924 (Tas) ss 130-130G

Victorian legislation

Legislation that can be used for cyberbullying or online threats:

Stalking

Crimes Act 1958 (Vic) s 21A

Legislation that makes it a criminal offence to bully in the workplace and it also covers cyberbullying between students:

Stalking (Brodie's Law)

Crimes Act 1958 (Vic) s 21A(D)

Legislation that can be used for sexting or child pornography offences:

Possess Child Pornography

Crimes Act 1958 (Vic) s 70

Manufacture Child Pornography

Crimes Act 1958 (Vic) s 68

Distribution of an Intimate Image

Summary Offences Act Sect. 41 (DA)1 41DB(3)

Threat to Distribute an intimate image

Summary Offences Act Sect. 41 (DB)1

Western Australian legislation

Legislation that can be used for cyberbullying or online threats:

Stalking

Criminal Code Act Compilation Act 1913 (WA) s 338E

Threats

Criminal Code Act Compilation Act 1913 (WA) s 338B

Production, Distribution or Possession of Child Exploitation Material

Criminal Code Act Compilation Act 1913 (WA) s 218-220

New Zealand legislation

Legislation that can be used for cyberbullying or online threats:

Threatening to kill or do grievous bodily harm

Crimes Act 1961 (NZ) s 306

Threatening to destroy property

Crimes Act 1961 (NZ) s 307

Misuse of telephone device

Crimes Act 1961 (NZ) s 112

Legislation that can be used for sexting or child pornography offences:

Produce or distribute objectionable publications

Films, Videos, and Publications Classification Act 1993 (NZ) s 123

Produce or distribute objectionable publications with the knowledge they are objectionable publications

Films, Videos, and Publications Classification Act 1993 (NZ) s 124

Possess objectionable publications

Films, Videos, and Publications Classification Act 1993 (NZ) s 131

Possess objectionable publications with the knowledge they are objectionable publications

Films, Videos, and Publications Classification Act 1993 (NZ) s 131A

CHAPTER 11

WHERE TO GO FOR HELP

It can be really difficult for a parent to know where to turn for advice and assistance, or simply to improve your knowledge about all things cyber. If you are not sure of what is what, then you can become extremely confused by the myriad of sites and blogs purporting to offer 'good' advice. Many, I am sure, are written with good intentions, but some contain dangerous advice. I have seen blogs that contradict legal requirements. Be extremely careful when looking for online advice. Just because a site, account or blog seems to have thousands of supporters or more, this does not mean the people behind it are experts or have any related qualifications. I have seen people called 'cybersafety experts' because they are tech-savvy or those who say, 'I'm a parent and I've dealt with it before.' These are admirable skills, but it doesn't make them experts.

Useful websites

The following websites contain a range of excellent information about a variety of online topics, issues and common areas of concern. I use them all and I have no hesitation in recommending them to you. Some contain similar information, just presented differently, so it will be a case of personal preference with some sites. Some, however, are unique. in what they offer. Many of the organisations have a presence on social media, so 'like' them on Facebook or follow them on Twitter to keep even more up to date. Others offer regular newsletters.

As many of the online problems that parents have to deal with involve other associated and compounding issues, I have included a further list of websites that will assist you should you need mental health advice after an incident has occurred, if you are just a bit worried about your child's changed moods or behaviour, or even if you're wondering what is considered 'normal' developmental behaviour.

All things cyber

aftab.com The website of Parry Aftab, a US lawyer, child advocate and expert in all aspects of cyber law, best practices, cyberbullying and cyber harassment, cybercrime and privacy. When Parry speaks, industry and government listen. The site is full of excellent information.

amf.org.au The website of the Alannah and Madeline Foundation and the home of the eSmart Schools Program. Lots of good information about general child safety as well as online abuse. Signing your school up for the eSmart school program is an excellent way to address the issue of cybersafety in schools.

bullying.org Established in 2000 by teacher and anti-bullying advocate Bill Belsey. The site contains good information about all bullying, including cyberbullying.

bullyingnoway.gov.au Australian Government anti-bullying website, which has information about all forms of bullying, including cyberbullying. The site includes links to the National Safe Schools Framework.

ceop.gov.uk The website of the Child Exploitation and Online Protection Centre UK, which is part of the National Crime Agency. World renowned in their work in the field of child online exploitation, the website is one of my favourites. It includes great information, the best videos and links to other useful sites. Follow on Twitter or Facebook for regular updates. Highly recommended.

commonsensemedia.org The website for Common Sense Media, dedicated to improving the lives of kids and families by providing the trustworthy information, education and an independent voice. This is a very useful site for parents, with reviews and ratings for games, apps, websites and more. Follow them on Twitter for regular updates direct to your phone.

communications.gov.au Australian Government website for all things digital. Visit the site to download the Cybersafety Help Button (which lets you access help and advice any time you need it) and for other useful information, including a comprehensive list of apps/websites and the relevant age restrictions.

cybersafetysolutions.com.au My website, with contact information, fact sheets and much more. The site also includes my contact details, as well as information about cybersafety education sessions and other services that I offer.

cybersmart.gov.au Australian Government cybersafety website. It includes information for kids, parents and educators, including fact sheets, research data and alerts on the latest online issues. There are also links to online reporting and other useful advice.

digizen.org Provides information for educators, parents, carers, and young people. The website is used to strengthen awareness and understanding of what digital citizenship is and encourages users of technology to be and become responsible digital citizens. There are good videos, and it also includes a fun activity called 'Social Networking Detective'. Download it and do it together with your kids; it's a great discussion starter about suitable social media profiles.

education.vic.gov.au The website of the Department of Education and Early Childhood Development in Victoria. Of particular note is the cyberbullying portal, where you will find useful information including fact sheets and online scenarios of common problems to work through. Click on the 'Bully Stoppers' icon on the main page to get to the correct part of the site.

esafety.gov.au Website of the Office of the Children's eSafety Commissioner. A one stop shop for all information for parents, carers, professionals, teachers and kids themselves. Also links to secondary reporting of online abuse content that a SM refuses to remove. Report offensive/illegal content as well.

getnetwise.org A public service website brought to you by the internet industry. Although based in Washington DC, GetNetWise has good, easy- to-understand and up-to-date information on a range of online issues, questions and concerns.

microsoft.com/security The safety and security section of the Microsoft website. This is a very valuable site if you are using a Microsoft product.

missingkids.com The website of the National Centre for Missing and Exploited Children (NCMEC), which was established in 1984. NCMEC is the leading non-profit organisation in the US working with law enforcement, families and the professionals who serve them on issues related to missing and sexually exploited children. All images of child abuse found in the USA and many other countries are sent to NCMEC for matching through their extensive database of identified victims. One of the leading agencies in the world, it is a good source of up-to-date information.

netsmartz.org An interactive, educational program of the National Center for Missing and Exploited Children (NCMEC) that provides age-appropriate resources to help teach children how to be safer on and offline. The NetSmartz Workshop program is designed for children aged five to seventeen years, parents and guardians, educators, and law enforcement. With resources such as videos, games, activity cards, and presentations, NetSmartz entertains while it educates. I love the games for kids on this site, and it is updated regularly.

netsmartz411.org An online resource about internet safety, computers, and the internet in general. There is a knowledge base for answers to many questions and an 'Ask the Experts' tab that lets you send them a question.

saferinternet.org.uk The UK Safer Internet Centre, coordinated by a partnership of three leading organisations: Childnet International, the South West Grid for Learning and the Internet Watch Foundation. There is lots of good information and you can sign up for regular newsletters or follow them on Twitter.

thinkuknow.co.uk An excellent cybersafety program initially designed to teach children about online predators, but now includes other online issues. While there is an Australian version, I prefer the information on the UK site. Be aware, however, that the Click CEOP reporting function is not valid here.

wiredsafety.org The largest and oldest online safety, education and help group in the world. Originating in 1995 as a group of volunteers rating websites, WiredSafety now provides one-to-one help, extensive information, and education to cyberspace users of all ages on myriad internet and interactive technology safety, privacy and security issues. While some information is USA-specific, most is relevant regardless of where you are from. It was founded by leading cybersafety expert and lawyer Parry Aftab (see earlier).

Mental health and general websites

blackdoginstitute.org.au The Black Dog Institute, a world leader in the diagnosis, treatment and prevention of mood disorders such as depression and bipolar disorder.

butterflyfoundation.org.au Website of the Butterfly Foundation, which represents all people affected by eating disorders and negative body image – a person with the illness, their family and their friends. Butterfly operates a national support line, staffed by trained counsellors experienced in assisting with eating disorders.

crimestoppers.com.au CrimeStoppers website. Report a crime or suspicious activity anonymously either online or via a dedicated telephone number.

eheadspace.org.au A confidential, free and secure space where young people twelve to twenty-five years or their family can chat, email or speak on the phone with a qualified youth mental health professional.

headspace.org.au The website for Headspace, the National Youth Mental Health Foundation, which provides help to young people who are going through a tough time. With fifty-five centres

around Australia, Headspace can help with general and mental
health, counselling, education, alcohol and other drug issues.

itstimewetalked.com.au Useful website for parents, teachers
and teens themselves to deal with the issue of access to
pornography.

kidshelp.com.au Kids Helpline, Australia's only free, private
and confidential telephone and online counselling service
specifically for young people aged between five and twenty-
five. The website has contact information for young people
and their parents/carers.

moodgym.anu.edu.au A free self-help program to teach cognitive
behaviour therapy skills to people vulnerable to depression
and anxiety.

oyh.org.au Orygen Youth Health (OYH), a world-leading youth
mental health organisation based in Melbourne, Australia. OYH
has three main components: a specialised youth mental health
clinical service; an internationally renowned research centre;
and an integrated training and communications program.

parentline.com.au Provides support, counselling and parent
education. Visit this site for the relevant links to the page
for your state or territory. It operates 8 a.m. to 10 p.m. seven
days per week.

psychology.org.au The Australian Psychological Society,
for a list of qualified psychologists listed by location and
field of expertise.

reachout.com.au Australia's leading online youth mental health
service. It's the perfect place to start if you don't know where
to look. On the site you will find fact sheets, stories and videos,
information on mental health issues, guides, tools, apps and
forums where you can connect with other young people

who have been there before, chat to experts and share your tips for health and wellbeing.

scamwatch.gov.au Part of the ACCC. This website gives great information on the latest scams, scams by type and how to report a scam.

theothertalk.org.au Website of the Australian Drug Foundation. It provides information for parents to assist them to have 'the other talk' about alcohol and other drugs. It's about letting your child know they can come to you to discuss not only drugs and alcohol, but also related issues such as peer pressure, health, parties, safety and expectations.

youthbeyondblue.com The young person–specific arm of beyondblue. beyondblue was established in October 2000 as a national five-year initiative to create a community response to depression. The aim was to move the focus of depression away from a mental health service issue and towards one that is understood, acknowledged and addressed by the wider community.

Books and publications

Who's Chatting to Your Kids?, Task Force ARGOS
Excellent brochure. Visit police.qld.gov.au /programs/cscp/ personalSafety/children/childProtection/ and download a copy.

Destroying Avalon, Kate McCaffrey
An absolutely true reflection of the insidious and often tragic consequences of cyberbullying. This is a must read for all teens and their parents. (Suitable for children in secondary school. I would advise that the parent/carer reads the book first.)

One Child at a Time, Julian Sher
A chilling read about how online predators think and act.

The content is confronting but it's well written and extremely informative.

Beyond Cyberbullying, Michael Carr-Gregg

The revised edition of Australia's leading adolescent psychologist Michael Carr-Gregg's 2007 book *Real Wired Child.*

Bully Blocking, Evelyn Field

One of Australia's leading bullying experts, psychologist Evelyn Field has written a book full of practical advice to help you help your child deal with bullying and teasing.

What's Happening to Our Boys? and

What's Happening to Our Girls?, Maggie Hamilton

Two fabulous books by Maggie Hamilton. Learn what our kids are exposed to and the impact it can have on them.

Raising Girls and **Raising Boys**, Steve Bidulph

The latest offerings by Steve Biddulph. Absolutely worth putting on the bookcase.

Big Porn Inc., Melinda Tankard Reist and Abigail Bray

A book that is powerful, confronting and downright scary in parts. If you have ever wondered what kids are looking at and why exposure to pornography is causing major problems, this book is for you. Do not let the internet be your child's sex educator.

Tech talk – a glossary

While I have attempted to minimise the amount of tech talk in this book, and have tried to explain each concept when covered, you will probably read about, hear of and see other things of which you're unsure of the meaning. This glossary is not a list of every single tech term, but it does attempt to cover the tech terms that I have used, those you are most likely to hear and those that will assist with your understanding of the tech world. This in turn can only assist you with the conversations you will be having with your children and will show them that you do have a level of understanding of all things cyber.

4G: The latest form of mobile phone technology that replaces what was called 3G. All 4G technology must provide peak date transfer rates of at least 100 Mbps.

acceptable use policy: A written policy that outlines and clearly defines the proper use and acceptable actions of people when using a particular computer or computer network. These policies are commonly found in schools and workplaces. As well as setting out clear guidelines for use, they should include examples of what is considered unacceptable and the range of penalties applicable if the policy is violated.

adware: A type of software that usually causes pop-up banners containing advertisements. When users click on the link provided, they are taken to another website. Sometimes these links contain viruses, so you should be very careful about clicking on any pop-up.

Android: A mobile operating system developed by Google. It is used by several brands of smart phones, such as Motorola and Samsung.

anti-virus software: A program used for scanning and removing viruses from your computer. Most have both automatic and manual scan options. Automatic scans check things as they are downloaded and/or opened, and they may also scan the entire hard drive on a regular basis. With the manual scan option you can choose to scan as required.

app: Short for 'application', which is the same thing as a software program. The term 'app' is most often used to describe programs for mobile devices, such as smart phones and tablets. The term was popularised by Apple when the company created the App Store in 2008. Many apps are free, but users can rack up large bills by making in-app purchases. Make sure you have in-app purchases set to off, or at least have them protected with a passcode your child does not know.

avatar: An internet user's representation of themselves within a virtual world, in a computer game (3D cartoon-type representation) or on a social networking site.

BitTorrent: A peer-to-peer (P2P) file-sharing protocol designed to reduce the bandwidth required to transfer files. This occurs because the file transfers are distributed across many systems. It makes the downloading of large movie or game files quicker and is often used to illegally obtain copies of the latest TV show, game or movie, as well as sharing them with others.

blocking/filtering software: A computer program designed to stop certain data from being seen by the person using the computer. It is most commonly used to limit what children can access on a computer at school or at home. Workplaces may also block access to certain sites such as social networking.

blog: Short for web log, a user-generated website where journal style entries are made and then displayed in a reverse chronological order. Blogs provide commentary or news on a particular subject and some function as personal online diaries. A typical blog combines both text and images and often allows the reader to leave comments in an interactive format.

bluetooth: Wireless technology that enables short-range communication between bluetooth-compatible devices using short wavelength radio transmissions.

broadband: Refers to the wide bandwidth characteristics of a digital transmission type. It has an ability to transport multiple signals and traffic types simultaneously. The two most common types are the DSL modem, which uses your existing phone line, and cable modems, which use the same connection as cable TV.

browser: A computer program that allows a computer user to access world wide web (WWW) pages on the internet. Some common browsers are Internet Explorer, Google Chrome, Safari and Mozilla Firefox. They read hypertext markup language (HTML) and display the web pages on the computer screen.

captcha: A program used to verify that a human, rather than a computer, is entering data. Captchas are commonly seen at the end of online forms, or on some internet banking logins. The user must enter the text exactly from a distorted image, some so difficult that several attempts are required. Most have an auditory feature as well so that those with poor eyesight can complete the task.

contact list: A list of internet chat friends, also known as a friends list. It allows you to be informed when one of your friends is online and ready to chat. It was first made popular with AOL's Instant Messenger system in 1997.

chat: Refers to an internet application that allows two or more people to carry on a text-based conversation in real time. Originally limited to typing messages (MSN), chat can now include voice and webcam communication. Chat functions are a common feature of social networking and gaming sites.

chat room: Can also be called a discussion group. It allows you to communicate in real time with either one or a group of people in the 'room'.

child pornography: The *Crimes Act* 1958 (Vic) defines child pornography as a file, photograph, publication or computer game that describes or depicts a person who is, or appears to be, a minor engaging in sexual activity or depicted in an indecent sexual manner or context.

cookie: Also known as an HTTP cookie, web cookie or browser cookie. It is a small piece of data sent from a website and stored in a user's web browser while the user is browsing that website. Every time the user loads the website, the browser sends the cookie back to the server to notify the website of the user's previous activity. An example of this is when you check the box 'remember me on this computer' so that the next time you log on you are either logged on automatically or you only have enter your password.

cloud computing: Also known as 'the cloud'. Imagine it as a computer hard drive that is accessible anywhere. It is where you save documents, music, addresses and so on, but instead of only being able to access it from the actual device, you can access all that material from any computer or internet-enabled device. It can be a problem, however, when your child stores inappropriate content in their cloud file rather than on the device itself, making it harder for you to check what they are up to.

cyberbullying: Can be described as any repeated harassment, insults and humiliation that occurs through the electronic mediums such as email, mobile phones, social networking sites, instant messaging programs, chat rooms and websites, and through playing online games.

cyberspace: The entire worldwide electronic communications system, which includes both small and large computer networks as well as the telephone systems.

discussion groups: A specific internet bulletin board. They are also referred to as newsgroups, listservs and forums.

domain name: A unique name that identifies a website. An example is www.cybersafetysolutions.com.au. This is the domain name of my company. Each website has a domain name that serves as an address, which is used to access the website. A domain suffix such as .com would indicate a commercial website, while .org would indicate a not-for-profit organisation. Some will end with a country code such as .au (Australia) or .uk (England), which lets people know where the website is based.

download: To copy a file from one computer system to another. Whenever you receive information from the internet, you are downloading it to your computer.

email: Short for electronic mail. Email is a store-and-forward method of composing, sending, storing and receiving messages using electronic communication systems. The term 'email' applies to both the internet (SMTP) and an intranet (internal) system within one organisation. Messages can be sent to single recipients or to multiple users. You can also attach word, picture, movie and music files.

email header: The data that is collected by an email as it travels from computer to computer. An email header can be very important in determining the true origin of an email. While it does not show up on the body of the email, it is easily found.

emoticon: The little text-based faces and objects that you often see in email, online chat and text messages. Initially limited to using symbols on a keyboard, such as :) for a smiley face, :D for a big smiley face, or :(for a sad face, it now includes actual tiny images to denote a range of emotions or celebratory events.

Facebook: The most popular social networking site in the world. The founders initially limited the website's membership to Harvard students, but it was expanded to other colleges in the Boston area, the Ivy League and Stanford University. It gradually added support for students at various other universities before opening to high school students, and eventually to anyone aged thirteen and over. Facebook users can create a profile with information about themselves, add pictures and videos and communicate with friends.

file: A collection of computer information.

filter: A product that manages what internet content is allowed to be viewed on a computer and manages the user's access to that content as well. Some filters allow for different people to have different levels of access on the same device; for example, children of different ages.

firewall: A software- or hardware-based network security system that controls the incoming and outgoing network traffic by analysing the data packets and determining whether they should be allowed through or not, based on a rule.

flaming: The act of posting or sending offensive messages over the internet. The messages, called 'flames', can be posted in online discussion forums or newsgroups, on social networking sites or on sites such as Twitter.

Flickr: Pronounced 'Flicker'. This is a popular website for sharing and embedding personal photos/images in blogs and social media.

Google: A popular internet search engine.

Google Drive: A file storage program that lets a user create a document, save it in the cloud, access the document anywhere online and share the document with others. Other authorised users can make changes to the document.

Google Play: A media player and media library application developed by Google that is used to play, buy, download and manage music and video on Chromebooks, Google and Nexus mobile devices, or devices running the Android operating system.

grooming: The process used by people who are sexually attracted to minors (paedophiles) to gain their victim's confidence and trust.

hacker: A person who gains unauthorised access to a computer, computer system or website by circumventing the security of the site or account.

handle: A pseudonym, the name you give yourself in an online chat, and often referred to as your screen name. If you decided to name yourself SexyJexy123, that would be your handle.

hard drive: The device that stores all your data. It houses the hard disk, where all your files and folders are physically located.

hardware: The physical components of a computer (keyboard, mouse, case, motherboard, etc.)

hashtag: A word or a phrase prefixed with the symbol #. The name 'hashtag' was coined by Twitter and combines the word 'hash' (another name for the number symbol) and 'tag', since it is used to tag certain words. For example, you can tag the word 'bully' in a tweet by typing '#bully'.

HDMI: Stands for 'high-definition multimedia interface'. HDMI is a digital interface for transmitting audio and video data in a single cable. It is supported by most high-definition TVs and things such as DVD and Blu-ray players, cable boxes and video game systems.

home page: The initial or front page of a website. This page usually describes the purpose of the site and has tabs and links that direct the user to other parts of the website.

host: A computer that serves data to another.

Hotmail: A free email computer system owned by Microsoft. It has recently been upgraded and is now called Outlook.com. All original Hotmail accounts can still be used.

HTML: Stands for hyper text markup language (HTML), the computer programming language that makes up the pages used on the world wide web (WWW).

HTTP: Hypertext transfer protocol (HTTP), the system that allows for data communication on the world wide web. This is why all website addresses begin with 'http://'.

HTTPS: Stands for hypertext transport protocol secure. HTTPS is the same thing as HTTP, but uses a secure socket layer (SSL) for security purposes. Some examples of sites that use HTTPS include internet banking, online shopping, airline bookings and most websites that require you to log in.

hyperlink: Also called a link. It is a reference to data that the reader can click on to go directly to another part of the website or another website altogether.

ICQ: Pronounced I seek you. This is a chat system that allows its users to chat, transfer files and interact with others.

ICT: Stands for information and communication technologies. These are technologies that provide access to information through the internet, wireless networks, mobile phones, tablets and all other kinds of communication.

IM: See *instant messaging*.

IMGUR: Pronounced 'imager'. This is an online image hosting service. Users can post directly to the Imgur gallery to allow the public to see it, add comments and vote.

Inbox: The main folder that your incoming mail gets stored in. Regardless of whether you access your mail through a webmail interface or use a program like Outlook or Mac OS X, each downloaded message gets stored in your inbox.

Instagram: An online photo-sharing, video-sharing and social networking app. Users can apply digital filters to pictures and videos and share them on social networking sites. It is now owned by Facebook.

instant messaging: Also called IM. This is a chat-like technology on an online service that allows instant (real-time) communication much like a phone call but via text. An example of this is MSN Messenger or Facebook Chat.

internet: A worldwide, publically accessible network of interconnected computer networks that transmit data by packet switching using the standard Internet Protocol (IP). It is a network of networks.

internet predator: A person who uses the internet to take advantage of others. Online predators are most often referred to when speaking of a person who is trying to locate and sexually abuse children using the internet.

iOS: A mobile operating system that was previously known as iPhone OS. It was developed by Apple Inc. and launched in 2007 for the iPhone, and is now used on other Apple devices such as the iPod Touch, the iPad, the iPad Mini and second-generation Apple TV.

IP: Stands for internet protocol. It is a set of rules for sending and receiving data over the internet. It is part of the term 'IP address'.

IP address: An Internet Protocol address(IP address). Every device (such as a computer or printer) that is part of a computer network using IP has one of these labels. An IP address is made up of four sets of numbers from 0 to 255, separated by three dots. An example IP address is 55.134.224.104.

Internet Relay Chat (IRC): A large internet chat network made up of many different networks.

internet service provider (ISP): A company that provides internet access to individuals and businesses, usually for a monthly fee.

internet stalking: The process of using computers and the internet to repeatedly and without authorisation contact, harass, annoy or frighten another person.

local area network (LAN): Two or more computers networked together, usually in the same area or building.

link: See '*Hyperlink*'.

LinkedIn: A professional networking website. LinkedIn lets you link to other professionals and share work-related information with them. You can create a business-related profile.

listserv: Software or hardware that provides an automated mailing list system allowing multiple people to receive the one email simultaneously.

Mac OS: The operating system that runs on Macintosh computers.

massively multiplayer online games (MMOG): An online video game that lets a large number of users to play on the internet simultaneously. An example is *World of Warcraft, or WoW*.

meme: A meme is a concept or behaviour that spreads from person to person. Examples of memes include beliefs, fashions, stories, and phrases. Some internet memes can be clever, but others are used to bully people.

metadata: Hidden data that provides information about an item. An image's metadata can describe the image's size, colour and resolution, and when and where it was created..

menu bar: A horizontal strip of available menus for a certain program. In Windows programs, the menu bar is at the top of each open window, while on the Mac, the menu bar is always fixed on the top of the screen.

Moodle: An acronym for Modular Object-oriented Dynamic Learning Environment. It is a free software e-learning platform originally developed to help create online courses. The first version of Moodle was released on 20 August 2002.

mouse: One of the primary input devices used with today's computers. It is a small mouse-shaped device that allows you to click and scroll on a computer. The tail of the mouse was initially represented by the cord but most are now connected via bluetooth so no cord is needed.

netiquette: Network etiquette. This is the rules and courtesy between people who use the internet. In other words, internet manners. An example is if you type a message or email in caps, then you are 'shouting' at the receiver.

network: Two or more computers linked together to share information.

newsgroup: An area of the internet where computer users can post messages including text graphics, photos and so on for others to see. The newsgroups are organised by thousands of different subjects.

operating system (OS): The software that acts as the interface between the computer user and the computer. Microsoft Windows, MacOS and Linux are all types of operating systems.

Outbox: Where outgoing email messages are temporarily stored. When the email message is compiled, it is then stored in the outbox until it is successfully sent to the recipient. Once the message has been sent, most email programs move the message to the 'Sent Messages' folder.

Outlook: A computer program developed by Microsoft for sending and receiving email. Outlook runs with the Microsoft Windows operation system.

P2P: Stands for 'peer to peer'. In a P2P network, the computers are connected to each other and can become both the server and the client as files can be shared in each direction. The traditional system is known as a client/server model.

packet: A series of characters of 'bytes' of data that is sent from one computer to another. On the internet, information is broken down into smaller packets of data and sent from one computer to another, where they are then put back together to form the original data.

parental controls: Computer software and/or hardware that allows parents to control some of the types of information that children are exposed to. It can also be used to limit access to certain apps, such games, camera or video sharing.

passcode/password: A series of letters, numbers and/or symbols that when placed in the correct order allow a person access to an area that is restricted from other users, such as logging on to an office computer or accessing your social networking account.

page view: Each time a user visits a web page, it is called a page view. Page views are also used in website analytics to see how many pages have been viewed on a website.

permalink: Short for 'permanent link'. A permalink is a URL that links to a web page or blog post. They give a specific

web address to each posting, which lets users bookmark blog
entries or link to them from other websites.

pharming: The malicious use of spyware or similar that is used
to redirect a website's traffic to another bogus site.

phishing: Involves sending an email that claims to be legitimate
in an attempt to scam the user into giving away private
information.

post: An electronic message that someone places in a newsgroup,
or on a social networking site or other internet group.

posting: Placing an electronic message to a newsgroup, social
networking site or other internet group. The message itself is
called a post.

Pinterest: A pin board–style photo-sharing website where you can
create and manage images. Users can browse other pin boards
for images, 're-pin' images to their own pin boards, or 'like'
photos.

POP3: Stands for 'post office protocol'. Sometimes called POP, this
is a standard method of delivering emails. A POP3 mail server
receives emails and filters them into the appropriate user
folders.

protocol: The set of rules and instructions by which computers
communicate with each other.

Reddit: A social news and entertainment website where registered
users submit content such as links or text posts. Other users
vote on the content, which then moves the post either up or
down the list. Content is sorted into areas of interest called
subreddits.

real time: An activity on a computer or the internet that happens
right now. An example of real-time communication is Skype,
or an instant messaging program such as Facebook Chat.

screen name: The name a person uses while on the internet.

screenshot: Also called a screen grab or screen capture. This is a picture taken of your computer, phone or tablet's screen, either as a whole or a particular open window. Screenshots are an easy way to save something you see on the screen, and important if you are going to report content to a school or police.

search engine: An internet computer program or website that allows a user to search the millions of internet sites for information. Some examples of common search engines are Google, Bing, Yahoo and Ask.

server: A computer that is programmed to accept requests for information and to provide (or serve) that information to authorised users. Servers are used for websites (web servers) and emails (email servers), and other internet activities.

sexting: Sending sexually explicit or naked messages or photos electronically, primarily between mobile phones, but can include internet applications such as instant messaging, email, photo/video sharing or social networking sites.

sextortion: A form of sexual blackmail in which sexual information or images are used to extort sexual favours or the payment of a sum of money from the victim. The term was coined by FBI agents investigating online blackmail cases where there was a sexual element to the case.

smishing: The term used to describe spam or fraudulent messages that come in via text messages (SMS).

SMTP: Stands for 'simple mail transfer protocol'. This is the protocol or rule used for sending email over the internet. Your email system uses SMTP to send a message to the mail server, and the mail server uses SMTP to relay that message to the correct receiving mail server.

social networking: Being part of a virtual community, for example on Facebook. Social networking sites provide users with simple tools to create a custom profile with text and pictures and to interact with each other. Sites can be set to be accessed by anyone (public) or restricted to a user's contacts (private).

software: The computer operating system (OS) that tells a computer what it is to do.

spam: The electronic equivalent of the junk mail that appears unsolicited in your letterbox, often sent in bulk transmissions of millions of messages at a time. Spam significantly slows the flow of legitimate internet traffic around the world.

spim: The version of spam that targets instant messaging (IM) services.

spit: The version of spam that can effect internet telephone such as VoIP programs (Skype).

sporn: Pornographic spam.

spyware: Software that helps gather information about a person or organisation without their knowledge. It may send that information to another person or allow them to remotely control your computer..

streaming: Data streaming; when a multimedia file can be played back without first being completely downloaded. The most common forms of streaming are that of audio and video.

tablet: A portable computer that uses a touch screen as its primary input device. Most tablets are smaller and weigh less than the average laptop. An on-screen, popup virtual keyboard is usually used for typing.

TOR: Originally an acronym for 'The Onion Router'. It is a method of diverting internet traffic so as to conceal the user's location or uses from others that may be spying on them. People engaging in illegal online activities often use it to try to avoid police investigations.

trojan horse: A hacking program that uses malware to gain access to an operating system without permission while appearing to be performing a desirable function. Trojans may cause the computer to run slowly. They can also steal information and cause damage to the user's device.

troll: A person who posts offensive, incendiary, or off-topic comments online. These comments may appear in web forums, on Facebook walls, in blog entries or in online chat rooms. Trolling commonly occurs on Twitter.

Tumblr: A blogging platform and social networking website owned by Yahoo! Inc. Users can post content to a short-form blog, follow other users' blogs, or make their blogs private.

tweet: An online posting or microblog created by a Twitter user. A tweet is limited to 140 characters in length.

Twitter: A microblogging site that allows users to post short pieces of information or comments known as tweets. Once you have created your account, you can post your own updates and view the updates others have posted. Once you are following a number of other users, their most recent tweets will show up on your home page. On the other hand, your tweets will show up on the home page of those who are following you. You can also tag a key word so that others looking for comment on the topic can easily find your tweet by giving it a 'hashtag'; for example, #Cyberspace tags the word 'cyberspace' on Twitter for others looking for tweets about cyberspace to find.

unfriend: When you remove a person from your friend list on a social networking site.

uniform resource locator (URL): The method of specifying a location for information on the internet. For example, the URL of the Australian Government's website is http://australia.gov.au.

upload: Transferring computer data from your computer to another computer system or network.

USB: Stands for 'universal serial bus'. The USB is the most common type of computer port used in today's computers. It can be used to connect keyboards, a mouse, game controllers, printers, scanners, digital cameras and removable media drives, just to name a few.

USB flash drive: A data storage device that includes flash memory with an integrated Universal Serial Bus (USB) interface. USB flash drives are typically removable and rewritable and used to store and transport data without the need to carry a large device.

VoIP: voice over internet protocol (VoIP), a technology that allows you to make voice calls using a broadband internet connection. Most now include a webcam facility so that you can see the person as well and allow multiple people to be involved at the same time.

virtual world: A computer-based simulated environment for its users to interact in. It can be themed, fantasy or with a parallel to the real world.

virus: An unwanted computer program that tries to attach itself to a person's computer software, usually without their knowledge, which, just like a virus in humans, makes the computer 'sick'. Like human viruses they have multiple 'symptoms' such as causing a computer to operate much slower than normal and in severe cases render it unusable.

webcam: The term webcam is a combination of 'web' and 'video camera'. The original purpose of a webcam was to post videos onto the web. Webcams were typically small cameras that attached to a user's monitor but now are an inbuilt part of the device (computer, phone or tablet). Webcams are used extensively in VoIP programs such as Skype, IM programs with camera facilities and in-video conferencing.

web history: The file where the locations of websites you've previously visited are listed.

webpage: Visual file of text and/or graphics that are found on the world wide web (WWW) and displayed on the user's computer, tablet or phone screen.

webmaster: The person in charge of maintaining a website.

website: A collection of related web pages.

Wiki: A website that allows users to add and update content on the site using their own web browser. This is made possible by wiki software that runs on the web server. The most common example of a large wiki is Wikipedia, a free encyclopaedia in many languages that anyone can edit. Many schools have class-based wikis that allow the students to add content to the one place.

WHOIS: An internet service that finds information about a domain name or IP address. If you enter a domain name into WHOIS, you are likely to be provided with information such as the name, address and phone number of the administrative, billing and technical contacts of the domain name.

WWW: World Wide Web. This is a system of interlinked hypertext documents accessed via the internet. Users navigate between web pages by clicking on hyperlinks.

YouTube: A video-sharing website on which users can upload and view videos. YouTube uses Adobe Flash Video and HTML5 technology to display movie TV clips music videos and various user-uploaded content such as video blogs and educational videos.

Internet abbreviations 101

Internet slang, which incorporates what we know as internet abbreviations or text speak, is the basis for many short, online, text-based communications. The origins were found in the earliest chat rooms, when users created their own 'shorthand' to communicate with other users. It was quick and simple and reduced the number of keystrokes required. These early 'online languages' have developed into the abbreviations now commonly found in popular instant messaging programs (IMs) such as Facebook Chat, Kik, and of course text messages on a mobile phone.

Many abbreviations are clever and fun; some, however, are used extensively by online predators to have a sexual conversation with a child so that even if a parent sees it, they would have no idea about what is being said. As a parent you need to know some of the abbreviations, so that when you get a text from your child you actually can understand what they are saying. Don't spend hours on this, but have a look and see if you already know some or use them without thinking. Just remember, if you see something on your child's account or phone that you don't understand, you can always google it.

2nite	Tonight
2moz	Tomorrow
AISI	As I see it

ASL	Age, sex, location
ASLP	Age, sex, location, pic
ALAP	As late as possible
BANANA	Penis
B4YKI	Before you know it
BF	Boyfriend
BFF	Best friends forever
BRB	Be right back
BRT	Be right there
BTW	By the way
BYAM	Between you and me
CEEBS	Can't be bothered
CCCO	Keep calm and carry on
CWYL	Chat with you later
CYA	See you
CYL8R	See you later
DBA	Don't bother asking
DILLIGAF	Do I look like I give a f**k
DUM	Did you masturbate
DUSL	Did you scream loud
DK	Don't know
DW	Don't worry
E123	Easy as one, two, three
EOD	End of day
F2F	Face-to-face
FFS	For f**k sake
FOMO	Fear of missing out
FONK	Fear of not knowing
FML	F**k my life
FOAF	Friend of a friend

G2G	Got to go
GF	Girlfriend
GNOC	Get naked on cam
Gr8	Great
GYPO	Get your pants off
H8	Hate
HAK	Hugs and kisses
ICUMI	In case you missed it
IDK	I don't know
IIT	Is it tight
ILY	I love you
IMHO	In my humble opinion
IMO	In my opinion
INBD	It's no big deal
IRL	In real life
ISS	I said so
JK	Just kidding
KIR	Keep it real
K	Okay
KK	Okay
KPC	Keeping parents clueless
KIT	Keep in touch
KITTY	Vagina
L8R	Later
LDR	Long-distance relationship
LMAO	Laughing my ass off
LMFAO	Laughing my f**king ass off
LMIRL	Let's meet in real life
LMK	Let me know
LOL	Laugh out loud

M8	Mate
M/F	Male or female
NIFOC	Nude in front of computer
NM	Not much
NMU	Not much, you?
N/P	No problem
NTK	Nice to know
OMG	Oh my god
OMFG	Oh my f**king god
OS	Oh shit
OSIF	Oh sh** I forgot
OTP	On the phone
PLZ	Please
PAL	Parents are listening
PAW	Parents are watching
PDA	Public display of affection
PIR	Parent in room
POS	Parent over shoulder
PPL	People
P911	Parents are coming
PRON	Porn
ROFL	Rolling on the floor laughing
RTFM	Read the f**king manual
RU	Are you?
RUH	Are you horny
RUOK	Are you okay
S2R	Send to receive (pic)
SOZ	Sorry
STFU	Shut the f**k up
SUP	What's up?
SWDYT	So what do you think

TDTM	Talk dirty to me
THX	Thanks
TS	Tough sh**
TTFN	Ta ta for now
TUVM	Thank you very much
TY	Thank you
T2UL8R	Talk to you later
YOLO	You only live once
YSVW	You're so very welcome
WE	Whatever
WFM	Works for me
WTG	Way to go
WT?	What the?
WTF	What the f**k?
WTGP	Want to go private
WUF	Where you from
8	oral sex
143	I love you
182	I hate you
420	marijuana
1174	nude club

ACKNOWLEDGMENTS

Sexts, Texts and Selfies is my first book, and I hope that it will provide all parents with much-needed practical advice to help them confidently parent in cyberspace.

First and foremost, I must thank Dr Michael Carr-Gregg, who I am honoured to say is both my friend and mentor. He believed in me from the start and helped me to believe in myself when others didn't. He also shares my passion for keeping children safe online. I am continually encouraged and supported by him every single day and I am eternally grateful for his friendship and advice.

To my publisher, Kirsten Abbott. I thank you for your patience, advice and enthusiasm for this book.

To the schools, parents and students who invite me into their world on a daily basis, a sincere thanks to you all!

The biggest thank-you of course must go to my family. I could not have done any of this without you. To my parents, who sadly are not here to read this book. You instilled in me the importance of helping those less fortunate and to speak up when something is not right. I hope you would be proud.

To my wonderful husband Ross. You have been with me every step of the way. You have never wavered in your support of me and my passion to keep children safe online. Thank you for your encouragement and for letting me follow my dreams. To my children Sarah, Adam and Luke ('Proofing's not fun, Mum.' Neither is getting you at 2 a.m.!). You are my inspiration. Together we have navigated cyberspace, learned from each other and come out the other side pretty much unscathed. You have patiently answered my questions and provided a young person's perspective to the book. Thank you, love you lots.